ADULT AUTISM SUPPORT GUIDE MADE SIMPLE AND EFFECTIVE

DEVELOPING COMMUNICATION, EMOTIONAL SUPPORT, AND SELF-AWARENESS

L. CELESTE

© **Copyright L. Celeste 2024—All rights reserved.**

The content within this book may not be reproduced, duplicated, or transmitted without direct written permission from the author or the publisher.

Under no circumstances will any blame or legal responsibility be held against the publisher, or author, for any damages, reparation, or monetary loss due to the information contained within this book. Either directly or indirectly. You are responsible for your own choices, actions, and results.

Legal Notice:

This book is copyright-protected. This book is only for personal use. You cannot amend, distribute, sell, use, quote, or paraphrase any part of this book's content without the author's or publisher's consent.

Disclaimer Notice:

Please note the information contained within this document is for educational and entertainment purposes only. All effort has been expended to present accurate, up-to-date, and reliable, complete information. No warranties of any kind are declared or implied. Readers acknowledge that the author is not engaging in the rendering of legal, financial, medical, or professional advice. The content within this book has been derived from various sources. Please consult a licensed professional before attempting any techniques outlined in this book.

By reading this document, the reader agrees that under no circumstances is the author responsible for any losses, direct or indirect, which are incurred as a result of the use of the information contained within this document, including, but not limited to—errors, omissions, or inaccuracies.

CONTENTS

Foreword — 7
Introduction — 11

1. UNDERSTANDING AUTISM IN ADULTS — 15
   The Spectrum Explained: Understanding the Diversity — 16
   Late Diagnosis: Challenges and Insights — 18
   Sensory Sensitivities: Recognizing Your Triggers — 20
   Executive Functioning in Adults with Autism — 23
   The Role of Empathy and Emotional Regulation — 26

2. PRACTICAL COMMUNICATION STRATEGIES — 29
   Mastering Body Language: A Guide for Better Interpretation — 29
   Recognize Common Gestures — 30
   Articulating Needs: Strategies for Clear Communication — 33
   Understanding and Using Tone and Inflection — 35
   Active Listening Skills for Enhanced Interactions — 38
   Navigating Misunderstandings in Communication — 40

3. BUILDING AND MAINTAINING RELATIONSHIPS — 45
   Starting Conversations: Practical Tips and Scripts — 46
   Maintaining Friendships: Understanding Reciprocity — 49
   Romantic Relationships: Finding and Sustaining Love — 52

Networking: Building Professional Relationships	56
Dealing with Conflict-Effective Resolution Strategies	59

4. DAILY LIVING SKILLS FOR INDEPENDENCE — 63
- Budgeting Basics: Managing Finances with Ease — 63
- Meal Preparation: Simple, Sensory-Friendly Recipes — 66
- Organizing Your Living Space for Sensory Comfort — 70
- Time Management Tools and Techniques — 72
- Personal Care Routines for Health and Hygiene — 75

5. NAVIGATING THE SENSORY WORLD — 83
- Designing a Sensory-Friendly Home — 83
- Coping Mechanisms for Public Places — 87
- Choosing Appropriate Clothing for Sensory Comfort — 90
- Creating a Personalized Sensory Diet — 96

6. MENTAL HEALTH AND EMOTIONAL WELL-BEING — 99
- Identifying Symptoms of Anxiety and Depression — 100
- Management Techniques That Work — 103
- Therapy and Counseling: Finding the Right Help — 107
- Self-Care Strategies for Emotional Resilience — 109
- Navigating Mental Health Services as an Autistic Adult — 112

7. ADVOCACY AND EMPOWERMENT — 115
- Understanding Your Rights as an Autistic Adult — 115
- Legal Rights and Autism: What You Need to Know — 125

8. FINDING AND BUILDING SUPPORT
   NETWORKS 129
   Online Support Networks: Connecting
   Digitally 129
   Local Support Groups: Finding the Right Fit 133
   Building a Support Network from Scratch 136
   Leveraging Social Media for Community
   Engagement 139
   Support for Families and Partners 143

9. SPECIAL INTERESTS AND PERSONAL
   DEVELOPMENT 149
   Identifying and Cultivating Special Interests 149
   Using Special Interests to Boost Career
   Opportunities 152
   Special Interests as a Coping Tool 156
   Balancing Special Interests with Daily
   Responsibilities 158
   Community Engaging Through Interests 160

10. MAKING THE MOST OF TECHNOLOGY 165
    Apps for Daily Organization and Task
    Management 166
    Technology for Nonverbal Communication 169
    Educational Tools for Continuous Learning 171

    Conclusion 177
    References 181

FOREWORD

Are you an adult with autism struggling to communicate your needs effectively?

Are you a caregiver seeking to understand better and support your loved ones?

Perhaps you're a professional aiming to provide tailored support to your autistic clients.

Imagine a world where autism is not a barrier but a gateway to profound self-awareness, a life of improved communication, and the attainment of emotional balance.

Although it might feel like you're walking an unbeaten path, unseen and unheard, you're not alone. Here's your chance to redefine your experiences in a world that often fails to understand honestly.

It introduces a groundbreaking guide that illuminates the complexities of autism, offering relatable insights and practical tools to empower adults on the spectrum, caregivers, and professionals alike.

Unlock a treasure trove of wisdom that includes:

- Strategies to manage sensory processing issues, enabling you to handle everyday encounters better
- Clear steps to enhance nonverbal and verbal communication, helping you articulate your needs effectively
- Techniques for building authentic connections and relationships, providing you with the comfort of a supportive community
- Indispensable advice on assertive self-advocacy, teaching you to stand up for your rights and needs
- Tactics to create and navigate online and local support networks, ensuring you never feel left out in the cold
- Practical guides on improving daily life skills, leading to an improved sense of independence
- Guidance on maintaining healthy romantic relationships, allowing you to cherish intimate connections without pressure
- Essential knowledge on seeking appropriate mental health support and advocating for your mental wellness
- Real-life coping strategies from autistic experts to tackle sensory overloads
- Inspirational stories of shared experiences illustrate that you are never truly alone in your journey

... and so much more!

Every individual with autism is unique, and this guide recognizes that. It offers a fresh outlook, integrating personal experiences and practical advice, enabling you to chart your path.

You might think, "I've tried reading such guides before, but they never seem to get what it's like for me." This book stands out with its focus on relatable and personalized experiences.

You might be concerned that the strategies are too challenging. Rest assured, each piece of advice is simplified and practical, facilitating easy application in daily life.

Perhaps you fear the book will be overly technical, drowning in medical jargon. This guide is perfectly balanced, maintaining a conversational tone that keeps you engaged from cover to cover.

You might object, "Every relationship advice I've read so far doesn't apply to someone with my level of social anxiety." This book offers empathetic and anxiety-friendly strategies to reassure and guide you.

If you're ready to embrace your autistic self, foster meaningful relationships, and live a life full of self-awareness, scroll up and click "Add to Cart."

INTRODUCTION

Welcome to a journey of understanding, support, and growth. As a mom with an adult son who has navigated the multifaceted world of autism for over thirty years, I've come to realize the profound need for a guide that speaks directly to adults with autism and those who support them. Our experiences have shaped my understanding and ignited a passion to help others find clarity and confidence in their paths.

This book is born from a deep-seated desire to offer hope and a practical toolkit for adults with autism. It's about embracing your unique perspective and acknowledging that how you see the world is not just okay—it's a remarkable strength. Here, you'll find strategies and a celebration of your identity, with all its challenges and opportunities.

My purpose is to provide the tools to help you understand the necessary ways to work through the complexities of adult autism. Whether you're building relationships, managing sensory overload, or advocating for yourself in a world that's often one step behind in understanding autism, this guide is here to support you. I'll explore these topics through a lens that respects and values your experiences, offering practical advice that you can tailor to your needs.

This is not your typical support guide. Here, we delve into real-life stories, including mine, to offer you solace and practical advice. Each chapter builds upon the latter, creating a comprehensive map for managing daily life, enhancing communication skills, and thriving in social and professional settings.

To my fellow people on this journey—the individuals with autism, their families, their friends, and their professionals—I write this for you. Your needs are as diverse as your experiences, and this guide aims to address those with care and precision. From understanding body language to navigating romantic relationships, this guide covers various essential topics with sensitivity and insight.

Let me assure you that the insights and strategies shared here are backed by thorough research and enriched with contributions from experts across the field of autism. My commitment to you is to provide a trustworthy and genuinely helpful resource.

As we turn these pages together, I invite you to embrace this guide as a partner in your journey. Take your time reading this to fully grasp how to understand who you are and find new strategies for connecting with others. Let's build a supportive community that celebrates neurodiversity, recognizing and valuing all individuals' abilities.

Together, let's step forward with hope, equipped with the knowledge and support to navigate the beautifully complex world of autism.

CHAPTER 1
UNDERSTANDING AUTISM IN ADULTS

When you hear the term autism, what springs to mind is perhaps a well-known character from a movie or a vignette shared in a popular book. While these snippets can offer glimpses into the autistic experience, they often fail to capture the rich, varied essence of living as an adult on the autism spectrum. This chapter is designed to deepen your understanding of autism, breaking through the surface level to explore the vibrant spectrum of experiences and traits that make up these unique people.

Autism is not a one-size-fits-all diagnosis; it's as diverse as the individuals it touches. Here, you'll find insights that reach beyond stereotypes, showcasing the strengths and challenges that those on the spectrum face. By weaving together scientific explanations with personal narratives, this chapter aims to provide a fuller, more nuanced understanding of what it means to be autistic. Whether you're someone with autism, a friend, a family member, or a professional working in supportive roles, these insights will equip you with a better understanding and appreciation of the autistic experience.

THE SPECTRUM EXPLAINED: UNDERSTANDING THE DIVERSITY

The language used to describe autism spectrum disorder has many layers—it highlights the vast range of differences among individuals with this diagnosis. The concept of a spectrum is a neurological and developmental disorder that affects how people interact with others, behave, learn, and communicate. Autism is described as a "developmental disorder" because the symptoms usually show up in the first two years of life. According to the Diagnostic and Statistical Manual of Mental Disorders (DSM-5), a guide created by the American Psychiatric Association that healthcare providers use to diagnose mental disorders, people with ASD share specific difficulties. For some, autism is a part of their identity that they celebrate, bringing skills and perspectives that are less common in the neurotypical population. For others, it presents significant challenges that require support and adaptation.

Autism is often depicted with narrow stereotypes, such as the inability to form relationships or possess savant skills like those portrayed in movies. However, these stereotypes are not only limiting but can also be misleading. Autistic adults form meaningful relationships, excel in various professional fields, and contribute uniquely to society, debunking the myth that autism is a barrier to personal achievement or emotional connection. It's crucial to understand that autistic adults might interact, communicate, or express affection in different ways, which are as valid as neurotypical expressions.

Many autistic individuals possess remarkable strengths due to their distinct neurological makeup. For instance, some have extraordinary memory skills, enabling them to remember detailed information and patterns. This can be advantageous in many professional and academic settings, where such precision and recall are invaluable. Others have heightened attention to detail, which can enhance their performance in fields like art, engineering, or data analysis. Honesty and loyalty are traits commonly found in the autistic community, valued in friendships and professional relationships.

Personal stories from adults on the spectrum offer a powerful lens through which to view these experiences. Consider the story of Melissa, an autistic graphic designer known for her exceptional attention to detail and innovative designs. While she faces challenges in social communication, her ability to see visual elements in extraordinary ways has made her a sought-after professional in her field. Or take Mark, whose memory of historical facts has turned him into a respected consultant for historical documentaries. These stories underscore the idea that if you've met one person with autism, you've indeed only met one person with autism. Each individual's abilities and challenges are unique portraits of life on the spectrum.

Interactive Element: Reflective Journaling Prompt

To further personalize your understanding of the diversity within the autism spectrum, take a moment to reflect on the following prompt in your journal: How does my experience or the experience of someone I know align with or differ from common stereotypes about autism? This exercise can help deepen your appreciation of the significant nature of autism and encourage a more personalized connection to the information shared in this chapter.

LATE DIAGNOSIS: CHALLENGES AND INSIGHTS

Being diagnosed with autism later in life can be a profound, sometimes disorienting experience. For many, this diagnosis comes after years of misunderstandings and misdiagnoses, bringing both challenges and a significant sense of relief. Navigating this new understanding of oneself involves rethinking past experiences and redefining personal identity, which can be both liberating and frightening. The revelation can explain previous difficulties in social situations, sensory sensitivities, or why specific interactions seemed more challenging than expected. However, it also raises questions about how to move forward with this new information.

One of the primary challenges of a late diagnosis is the reformation of one's identity. Adults might reflect on their life experiences through a new point of view, questioning past relationship difficulties, job challenges, or educational barriers. This can lead to a re-evaluation of self-perception, which, while ultimately healing, can initially cause confusion and isolation. Another significant challenge is coping with past misunderstandings. Many adults may look back on their school years or early careers and recognize missed opportunities for support. They might recall instances where their behavior was misinterpreted as intentional or disruptive rather than a communication of unmet needs or sensory overload.

Despite these challenges, a late diagnosis of autism also brings considerable benefits. The foremost among these is self-understanding. By knowing they are on the spectrum, individuals can better understand their reactions, preferences, and needs. This understanding is empowering—it can foster a greater sense of self-compassion and pave the way for asking for what they genuinely need to thrive. Additionally, a diagnosis opens access to targeted support services. These services can significantly improve quality of life, from occupational therapy designed to improve daily functioning to counseling that can help process a lifetime of misunderstood interactions. Also, you need support from a job coach, funding for social interactions, and a person who works directly with you and your family to meet your individual needs—leading into how to navigate the health care system.

A new diagnosis of autism requires knowledge and advocacy. It's crucial to find healthcare providers and specialists who understand adult autism, which can be a hurdle, as many services are tailored to children. Finding the proper support often involves a combination of research and outreach. You may need to speak with multiple professionals to find someone who understands your needs and can offer the appropriate support. Advocating for oneself becomes essential during this process. Being clear about your needs, asking questions, and sometimes even educating healthcare providers about adult autism can ensure you receive the best possible care. Having a family member, friend, or case manager can help you determine a plan to meet your needs.

Coping with the emotional impact of a late diagnosis is another critical area. Many adults benefit from therapy, where they can explore their feelings about the diagnosis and learn strategies for managing anxiety or depression that might accompany this new understanding of themselves. Joining support groups in person or online can also be incredibly beneficial. These groups provide a sense of community and belonging, allowing individuals to share experiences and strategies with others who truly understand what it's like to discover one's autistic identity later in life. These coping strategies help manage the immediate emotional impacts of a diagnosis and support long-term well-being and personal growth.

SENSORY SENSITIVITIES: RECOGNIZING YOUR TRIGGERS

Understanding how sensory processing affects you is crucial in navigating everyday life with autism. Sensory processing issues can profoundly influence daily activities, often more than people realize. For many autistic adults, the world is experienced in high definition—every sound, light, and texture is amplified. This heightened awareness can be both a gift and a challenge, depending on the environment and the situation. By exploring the nature of these sensory experiences, you can learn to manage them effectively, reducing discomfort and enhancing your ability to engage with the world and others. This is usually a work in progress. Others who are close to you can often help you identify your triggers.

Sensory processing refers to how our brains interpret and respond to sensory information. For someone on the autism spectrum, this process can often be overwhelming, as the brain may have difficulty filtering out irrelevant sensory data. This can lead to what many describe as sensory overload, where everyday environments feel unbearably intense or distracting. Common triggers for sensory overload include loud noises, such as traffic or alarms, which can seem louder and more distressing. Also, these sounds may vary in intensity at different times of the day.

Bright lights can be piercing and uncomfortable, leading to headaches or irritability. Even certain textures, like those of woolen clothes or tags in clothing, can feel unbearable on the skin.

Creating a sensory-friendly environment is about minimizing these triggers. At home, this might mean using soft, natural lighting instead of harsh fluorescents or investing in noise-canceling curtains in urban areas to dampen street noise. Decluttering the home, especially where the individual is most in —for example, their bedroom if cluttered by mementos—can reduce sensory overload. In the workplace, you could arrange a quiet space away from the bustle of open-plan offices or request accommodations to work from home on days when your sensory sensitivities are particularly acute. These adaptations reduce sensory overload and help maintain focus and productivity, making daily tasks more manageable and less exhausting. The key is to know and understand what triggers you.

In addition to adjusting your environment, personal adaptation techniques are vital in handling sensory sensitivities. Noise-canceling headphones are a fantastic investment, allowing you to control auditory input and protect yourself from unexpected noises that could cause distress. Sunglasses or tinted lenses can help manage light sensitivity, making outings and bright environments more comfortable. For tactile sensitivities, choosing clothing made from soft, natural fabrics without irritating seams or tags can make a significant difference in your comfort throughout the day.

Textual Element: Checklist for Creating a Sensory-Friendly Environment

- **Lighting**: Replace fluorescent bulbs with soft white or adjustable LED lights.
- **Acoustics**: Use rugs, curtains, and wall fabrics to reduce echo and external noise.
- **Furniture**: Choose smooth textures and rounded edges for comfort and safety.
- **Personal Comfort Items**: Keep items like weighted blankets or stress balls accessible to help manage sensory needs.

These adaptations and techniques are about minimizing discomfort and empowering you. By understanding and managing your sensory triggers, you can create a balanced environment that supports your well-being and allows you to thrive. Whether at home, work, or in social settings, these strategies provide a foundation for navigating the world in a way that respects your unique sensory needs.

EXECUTIVE FUNCTIONING IN ADULTS WITH AUTISM

Executive functioning is a set of cognitive processes necessary to control various behaviors. This is a series of mental processes that are crucial for controlling and managing behavior and thoughts. This includes everything from planning and organizing to task initiation and switching focus between activities. For adults with autism, often knowing what's expected of them ahead of time will help. For example, letting them know that they need to do a particular task and giving them time to process what is required makes the transition much smoother. Challenges in executive functioning can often manifest as difficulties in these areas, impacting daily life and the ability to achieve personal and professional goals. Understanding and managing these challenges is critical to enhancing overall functionality and independence.

For many adults on the spectrum, initiating tasks can be particularly challenging. This often stems from difficulty breaking down a task into manageable steps or an overwhelming uncertainty about how to start. Switching focus can also be tricky; shifting to another activity can feel disruptive and disorienting once engaged. This is further compounded by difficulties in organizing tasks, making managing daily responsibilities feel like navigating a labyrinth without a map.

Addressing these challenges begins with establishing clear, manageable steps. One strategy that helps many people is to use visual aids, such as charts or checklists, to clarify what needs to be done and when each day. These tools provide a visual reminder of tasks and help break down larger projects into smaller, more manageable parts. This can significantly reduce the anxiety accompanying task initiation, making starting and maintaining momentum easier.

Setting alarms is another practical tool for those with executive functioning difficulties. Alarms can serve as reminders for starting or switching tasks and can be put on devices most of us already use, such as smartphones or tablets. When using this tool, you can set the sound to a soothing sound so it doesn't upset you. This method helps maintain a routine, ensures that time is allocated effectively across tasks, and minimizes the risk of getting overly absorbed in one activity to the detriment of others. For example, setting alarms throughout the day can prompt an individual to begin a work assignment, take a necessary break, or transition to household chores, thereby balancing productivity and rest.

Breaking tasks into smaller steps is crucial for individuals with executive functioning challenges. This approach makes tasks seem less challenging and provides a clear pathway to completion. It's about changing the perception of a task from a mountain to a series of small, achievable hills. For instance, if a project requires research, writing, and editing, each component can be tackled separately with breaks in between, making the overall task more approachable and less overwhelming.

Tools and Apps to Assist with Executive Functioning

In today's digital age, various tools and apps are specifically designed to assist with planning, time management, and reminders. These can be particularly beneficial for adults with autism, offering support that is both accessible and customizable to fit individual needs and preferences. For example, apps like Trello or Asana allow users to organize tasks into customized boards and lists, making it easy to see what needs to be done at a glance. These tools also offer features like setting deadlines, reminders, and adding notes or subtasks, which can help manage complex projects or daily to-dos.

Another invaluable tool is a digital calendar, such as Google Calendar, which can schedule one-time and recurring tasks. This helps keep track of appointments and deadlines and establishes a routine, which can be very stabilizing. Calendars can be synced across multiple devices, ensuring that reminders are always accessible at home, at work, or on the go.

For those who benefit from real-time task management, apps like Forest offer an innovative solution. This app encourages focus by letting you grow a virtual tree, which will wither if you leave the app to check social media or perform other distracting activities. It's a visual and interactive way to manage time and maintain focus on the tasks at hand.

Moreover, simple tools like alarm clocks or timers can help manage time effectively. Setting a timer for the tasks that need to be done can help ensure you spend the appropriate amount of time on each activity without losing focus or getting sidetracked. This can be particularly helpful for less engaging tasks, as it provides a clear endpoint to the activity, after which a more enjoyable task can be tackled.

Incorporating these tools into daily life can significantly ease challenges. By leveraging technology and adopting structured methods, adults with autism can strengthen their ability to plan, execute, and manage tasks, leading to a more organized and fulfilling life. Whether through visual aids, digital tools, or simply breaking tasks into smaller parts, the goal is to create a supportive structure that promotes independence and success in daily activities.

THE ROLE OF EMPATHY AND EMOTIONAL REGULATION

One of the most common myths about autism is the belief that autistic individuals lack empathy. This misconception stems from a misunderstanding of how empathy manifests in different people. Empathy typically involves two main components: cognitive empathy, which consists of knowing how people think and feel, and the ability to understand another person's perspective or mental state. Emotional empathy involves feeling another person's emotions. For many autistic adults, the challenge lies not in experiencing empathy but in the ways they express it. They might understand someone's distress (cognitive empathy) but not display a typical emotional response (affective empathy). This difference doesn't mean empathy is absent but rather that it is communicated in ways that might not align with conventional expectations.

Emotional regulation is another complex area for many autistic adults. This term refers to how we influence our emotions when we have them and how we experience and express them. Autistic individuals might experience emotions more intensely or have difficulty moderating their responses to emotional stimuli. This heightened sensitivity can often be linked to sensory sensitivities—a crowded room isn't just a space filled with people; it's an overwhelming barrage of sounds, sights, and smells that can trigger an intense emotional response. Understanding these connections is crucial in developing effective strategies for managing emotions.

Techniques to enhance empathy and improve emotional expression can be invaluable. Role-playing, for example, provides a safe environment to practice social interactions and explore both cognitive and affective empathy. By simulating different social scenarios, autistic adults can learn to recognize and respond as needed to social cues, improving their ability to communicate empathy in ways that are understood by others. Similarly, mindfulness practices can help develop a greater awareness of one's emotions, the first step in effective emotional regulation. Practices such as focused breathing, meditation, or mindful walking encourage active, open attention to the present. When practiced regularly, mindfulness can help decrease the intensity of emotional responses by fostering a state of calm and centeredness.

Coping mechanisms for emotional regulation are vital for managing fierce emotions arising from everyday stressors or sensory overload. Problem-solving can empower autistic adults to address emotional triggers directly. This might involve identifying the problem, brainstorming possible solutions, evaluating them, and implementing them. For instance, if a noisy environment is causing stress, solutions might include using noise-canceling headphones or finding a quieter location. Also, deep breathing, progressive muscle relaxation, or visualization can provide immediate relief in stressful situations. These practices help shift the body's response from a state of arousal to relaxation, making it easier to manage overwhelming emotions.

Navigating the complexities of empathy and emotional regulation requires patience and practice. It involves understanding the unique ways in which autistic adults experience and express their emotions and developing tailored strategies to support their emotional well-being. By fostering better understanding and effective coping mechanisms, autistic adults can enhance their interpersonal relationships and improve their overall quality of life. This empowerment through self-awareness and skill development is a critical step in embracing the full spectrum of experiences that come with autism.

CHAPTER 2
PRACTICAL COMMUNICATION STRATEGIES

As we delve into the intricacy of communication, it's essential to recognize that for many of us, especially those on the autism spectrum, navigating the maze of social interactions isn't just about the words we use. It's about understanding a whole other language—body language. This chapter aims to enlighten and equip you with the tools to interpret better and use body language, enhancing your ability to communicate and connect with the world around you.

MASTERING BODY LANGUAGE: A GUIDE FOR BETTER INTERPRETATION

Body language speaks volumes, often saying more than words ever could. Understanding these nonverbal cues might not come naturally to you, making social interactions confusing or even stressful. Let's break down these barriers by exploring common gestures and expressions, offering insights into what people might communicate.

We'll also touch upon how cultural variations can influence body language interpretations and provide tips on expressing yourself more clearly through your body language.

RECOGNIZE COMMON GESTURES

You encounter countless facial expressions and gestures daily at a café, office, or during a casual walk in the park. A smile, a frown, or a shrugged shoulder can convey distinct emotions and intentions. Understanding these can be key to learning a new language. For instance, crossed arms can indicate a person is defensive or closed off, but it might simply mean they are cold sometimes. A nod, on the other hand, generally means agreement or acknowledgment. By familiarizing yourself with these common gestures, you unlock the silent messages people send, which can be particularly empowering in personal and professional interactions.

Practice Scenarios

Practicing scenarios is a valuable tool in improving your ability to interpret nonverbal cues. Imagine you are at a social event. You see a group of people laughing, with one person's eyes squinted, lips wide in a smile, head tilted slightly. What do you think they're feeling? Joy, perhaps amusement. By setting up similar mental scenarios or even using flashcards with pictures of different facial expressions and body postures, you can train yourself to interpret these cues more effectively. This practice can boost your confidence and magnify your ability to interact smoothly, making social environments less intimidating.

Body Language in Different Cultures

Understanding body language in different cultures is essential. It's fascinating how cultural contexts can shape how body language is expressed and interpreted. In some cultures, direct eye contact is seen as a sign of respect and attention; in others, it might be perceived as confrontational. Awareness of these cultural differences is crucial, especially in our increasingly globalized world. It helps prevent misunderstandings and builds more respect and understanding across diverse groups. This knowledge is particularly valuable if you find yourself in multicultural settings or if you love traveling and experiencing new cultures.

Improving Personal Body Language

Now, turning the lens inward, how can you use body language to enhance your communication? Simple adjustments can significantly impact how others perceive and respond to you. If maintaining eye contact feels too intense, try focusing on the space between someone's eyes or their forehead—it still conveys engagement without discomfort. Hand gestures can also help you emphasize your points and express your emotions more clearly. Practice these in front of a mirror or record or video yourself to see how others might perceive your gestures and expressions. This helps make your nonverbal cues more effective and boosts your confidence in expressing yourself. Repetitiveness is essential to familiarizing yourself and remembering the skills.

Textual Element: Body Language Quick Reference Guide

- **Smile**: Indicates happiness, friendliness, or agreement. It can vary in intensity; a slight smile may be polite, while a broad smile shows genuine pleasure.
- **Eye Contact**: Shows attentiveness and interest. Lack of eye contact might indicate nervousness, distraction, or, in some cultures, respect.
- **Crossed Arms**: These are often seen as a sign of resistance or defensiveness, but they can also mean the person is simply comfortable in that position or cold.
- **Nodding**: Usually signifies agreement or acknowledgment. Rapid nodding can imply eagerness or impatience to add to the conversation.
- **Hand Gestures**: Emphasize speech; the style and extent can vary widely across different cultures.

Mastering the art of body language opens a new dimension of communication. It allows you to interpret others' intentions and emotions better and express your own more clearly. This skill enhances your interactions and relationships, making social situations more navigable and less intimidating. Whether engaging in a casual chat or a formal meeting, the ability to read and use body language effectively can be a game-changer, empowering you to communicate confidently and clearly.

ARTICULATING NEEDS: STRATEGIES FOR CLEAR COMMUNICATION

Communicating your needs and thoughts effectively can sometimes feel like navigating a maze without a map, mainly when interactions don't always go as planned due to misunderstandings or misinterpretations. This section will equip you with the tools to express your thoughts and needs clearly and confidently, ensuring your voice is heard and understood personally and professionally.

Structure Your Thoughts

Organizing your thoughts before a conversation can significantly improve clarity and prevent misunderstandings. One effective way to do this is through mind mapping. This technique helps you organize information visually, making it easier to track and articulate your thoughts during discussions. Start with a central idea and branch out into subtopics or related points. This helps keep track of your discussion points and ensure you cover all necessary aspects without getting sidetracked. Bullet points can also be a practical tool, especially in professional settings where key points must be concise and impactful. Before meetings or essential conversations, jot down bullet points of the topics you wish to cover. This preparation ensures you don't forget critical elements and helps maintain a logical flow in your communication.

Assertion Techniques

Asserting yourself in conversations is crucial, especially when communicating needs and boundaries. However, it's essential to do so in a way that is respectful yet firm. One method is using "I" statements. Instead of saying, "You make me feel ignored," try, "I feel ignored when I'm not included in decision-making." This phrase focuses on your feelings rather than accusing others, which can reduce defensiveness and open the conversation for more constructive dialogue. Another technique is maintaining a calm and steady tone, even when the discussion becomes challenging. This will help keep the conversation productive and focused on resolution rather than conflict. When this situation arises, take a moment and take a deep breath, which signals the body to relax. You may need to do this several times, depending on the situation.

Role-Playing Exercises

Role-playing can be an invaluable tool for practicing communication skills. By simulating different scenarios, you can develop the confidence to express your needs and handle various responses. For instance, role-play a scenario where you need to ask for a deadline extension from a supervisor. Practice different approaches and anticipate possible responses. This not only prepares you for the actual conversation but also helps in refining your communication style. Engaging in these exercises with a trusted friend or mentor can provide feedback and different perspectives, enhancing your learning experience.

Feedback Loops

Feedback loops are essential in ensuring your message is understood as intended. After expressing your thoughts or needs, encourage the other person to paraphrase or summarize what they've heard. This practice confirms that your message has been received correctly and allows you to clarify any points that may have been misunderstood. If the feedback indicates a discrepancy, calmly provide the necessary clarifications. Establishing this kind of two-way communication fosters understanding and minimizes the chances of misunderstandings escalating into conflicts.

Integrating these strategies into your communication practices can transform your interactions, making them more effective and fulfilling. Whether dealing with colleagues, friends, or family, articulating your needs clearly and confidently is a powerful skill that enhances your relationships and contributes to your overall well-being. As you continue to apply these techniques, you'll likely find that your needs are better understood and that you are more adept at navigating the complex landscape of human interaction, equipped with the tools to express yourself authentically and effectively.

UNDERSTANDING AND USING TONE AND INFLECTION

Tone and inflection are the unsung communication heroes, often carrying as much weight—if not more—than the words themselves. Think about how a simple phrase like I can't believe you did that can be expressed in numerous ways. Said with a light, pleasant tone, it can express amusement or mild surprise. However, the exact phrase uttered with a sharp, harsh tone might convey anger or disapproval. This subtle art of inflection can significantly alter the message's impact, making it crucial to master both interpreting and using tone effectively in your interactions.

The Role of Tone in Communication

Let's delve into how tone can influence communication. Imagine listening to two audio clips where someone says, "We need to talk." In the first clip, the speaker's voice is calm, even, and slightly soft. The voice is lower, slower, and perhaps colder in the second. The first might make you curious or mildly concerned but likely still at ease. The second, however, might spark anxiety or a sense of impending trouble. This experiment highlights how tone can completely change the perceived intent behind words. You can better gauge others' emotions and responses by tuning into these variations, allowing for more empathetic and effective communication.

Modulating Your Tone

Learning to modulate your tone to align with your emotional intent is invaluable, particularly when you aim to communicate your feelings clearly and avoid misunderstandings. Here's a simple exercise to practice this: Record yourself saying the sentence: 'I appreciated that ..."—several times, each with a different emotional undertone—gratitude, sarcasm, surprise, and indifference. Play back the recordings and listen carefully. How does your tone change with each emotion? How might others interpret each variation? This exercise helps you become more aware of how you use tone and enhances your ability to adjust it consciously, ensuring your verbal expressions match your intentions.

Interpreting Others' Tones

Interpreting the tone of others can be particularly challenging, especially in nuanced or emotionally charged conversations. To improve this skill, focus on listening to the words being said and how they are being told. Pay attention to the pitch, pace, and volume changes—these often provide clues about the speaker's true feelings. For instance, a sudden increase in pitch might indicate excitement or anxiety, while a volume drop could indicate sadness or disappointment. Practice by watching films or shows with the sound turned off initially, then replaying the same scene with sound. Observe how tone gives context to the emotions and intentions behind the dialogue, enhancing your ability to read between the lines in real-life interactions.

The Impact of Digital Communication

Misunderstandings are frequent in texts and emails, where tone can't be heard. Digital communication strips away the intentions conveyed through voice, making it easy to misinterpret the sender's intent and use emoticons to clarify your tone or explicitly state your emotions to mitigate this. Phrases like "I'm genuinely curious or thrilled to announce" can help convey your feelings more clearly. When interpreting digital communications from others, if the tone seems ambiguous or the message evokes a strong emotional reaction, it may be helpful to ask for clarification before jumping to conclusions. This approach helps prevent misunderstandings and maintains positive, clear communication channels, even in a digital format.

Navigating the subtleties of tone and inflection enhances your communication ability and deepens your relationships as you become better equipped to understand and meet others' emotional needs. These skills are integral to building more robust, empathetic connections in every interaction, whether adjusting your tone to convey your feelings better or interpreting the emotional undertones in others' voices.

ACTIVE LISTENING SKILLS FOR ENHANCED INTERACTIONS

Active listening is not just about hearing the words spoken but truly understanding and engaging with the speaker. This skill is fundamental in all relationships and interactions, fostering mutual respect and understanding. It involves more than just listening; it's about attention, interpretation, and response. Key components include maintaining eye contact, nodding to show engagement, and paraphrasing what has been said to ensure clarity and understanding. Each action signals to the speaker that you are fully present and genuinely interested in the conversation, which can significantly deepen the connection between you and the speaker.

Maintaining eye contact, for example, shows that you are focused and attentive. However, it's crucial to balance this so it remains comfortable for both parties—sometimes, especially for individuals on the autism spectrum, too much eye contact can feel overwhelming. Finding a comfortable gaze point, perhaps on the bridge of the nose or near the eyes, can help maintain the right balance. Nodding occasionally shows that you follow along and encourages the speaker to continue. On the other hand, paraphrasing involves repeating what the speaker has said in your own words, which can clarify any misunderstandings immediately and show that you are actively processing the information shared.

However, several barriers can impede effective listening. Distractions are a common challenge. In today's digital age, notifications from smartphones or computers can easily pull your attention away from the conversation. Creating a physical environment conducive to listening, such as turning off screens or moving to a quieter space, can help mitigate these distractions. For autistic individuals, literal interpretations can also pose a challenge. Sometimes, phrases or idioms don't mean precisely what they say, and learning to interpret these situations is a crucial part of active listening. This can be improved through practice and, if needed, explicit explanations of such phrases during conversations with understanding partners.

Engaging in practical exercises can be very beneficial for enhancing your listening skills. For instance, audio-based quizzes that require you to listen to a conversation and then answer questions about it can sharpen your ability to catch details and understand the underlying message. Another effective exercise is to practice conversing with a partner, where you take turns speaking and listening. The listener can then summarize what was said to check their understanding. This practice improves not only listening skills but also builds confidence in interpersonal interactions.

Being a good listener can transform your relationships and interactions. It allows for more transparent communication and reduces the likelihood of misunderstandings, which is particularly important in negotiations or discussions with high stakes. Furthermore, active listening shows respect and care for the speaker, qualities that are deeply valued in all relationships. Whether in a professional setting, among friends, or with family, being known as a good listener can strengthen your connections with others and open new avenues for collaboration and understanding. This skill, once developed, can significantly enhance your social interactions and lead to more positive outcomes in all areas of communication.

NAVIGATING MISUNDERSTANDINGS IN COMMUNICATION

Misunderstandings are inevitable in human interactions, but knowing how to navigate them effectively can significantly enhance your communication skills and relationship management. Various factors contribute to misunderstandings, ranging from ambiguous language to cultural nuances, each adding complexity to everyday exchanges. By exploring these factors and learning strategies to address and resolve misunderstandings, you can foster more precise and effective communication in all areas of your life.

Common Causes of Misunderstandings

Misunderstandings can arise from various scenarios, often involving unclear language or assumptions based on cultural backgrounds. Ambiguous language leaves room for interpretation, which can diverge significantly from the speaker's original intent. For instance, a simple statement like "I'll do it soon" can vary widely in meaning based on one's definition of soon—from a few minutes to several days. Cultural differences can further complicate communications. Social norms that dictate conversational styles, such as the directness of speech or the appropriateness of topics, vary widely across cultures. For someone from a culture where direct communication is valued, indirect hints or suggestions may go unnoticed, leading to confusion and unmet expectations.

Personal biases and emotional states also significantly influence how messages are sent and received. People who are stressed or preoccupied may not communicate their thoughts clearly or misinterpret what others say. Similarly, if you have had previous conflicts with someone, you might be more inclined to interpret their comments negatively, regardless of their actual intent. Awareness of these dynamics can help you approach conversations with a clearer understanding of what might go wrong and how to steer them toward mutual understanding.

Strategies for Clarification

When misunderstandings arise, seeking clarification calmly and openly can prevent the situation from escalating. One effective method is to use open-ended questions that encourage detailed responses rather than yes or no answers. For example, if someone says, "I'm upset with your work," you might respond with, "Can you explain what aspects of my work concern you?" This shows your willingness to understand and provides a clear framework for the conversation to proceed constructively.

Reflective listening is another powerful tool. This involves paraphrasing what the other person has said to confirm your understanding. If there's a discrepancy between what was intended and what you understood, this technique allows immediate correction and clarification. For example, "Do you need the report by tomorrow morning?" This approach helps ensure that both parties are on the same page, reducing the likelihood of further misunderstandings.

Repairing Misunderstandings

Once a misunderstanding is recognized, taking steps to repair the relationship is crucial. Apologizing sincerely if you were at fault or if your words were misinterpreted can go a long way in mending relationships. It's essential to be specific about what you are apologizing for and to express a genuine desire to avoid similar issues. For example, saying, "I apologize for not making my expectations clear; I will make sure to specify deadlines in the future," shows that you are taking responsibility and are committed to improving your communication.

Rebuilding trust is equally important and can be achieved by consistently communicating clearly and reliably and following through on commitments. Demonstrating that you are learning from past errors and making efforts to prevent them reassures others of your commitment to a positive and constructive relationship.

Preventative Measures

Setting clear expectations from the beginning of any conversation or project is key to reducing the frequency of misunderstandings. Clearly defining roles, deadlines, and requirements can prevent ambiguity. Additionally, confirming understandings through follow-up emails or messages can provide a written record of what was agreed upon, which can be helpful for reference and clarification.

Adopting these strategies minimizes the frequency and impact of misunderstandings and enhances one's capability to interact harmoniously and effectively with others. As one continues to apply these techniques, they will likely find that relationships—at work, home, and social life—become more stable and satisfying, paving the way for deeper connections and more successful collaborations.

As we wrap up this chapter on enhancing communication strategies, remember that the journey toward becoming a more effective communicator is ongoing. Each conversation offers a new opportunity to apply and refine these skills. The more you engage with others, the easier it will become to be a better communicator. Next, we will explore how to build and maintain relationships, a crucial aspect of personal and professional life that relies heavily on the foundations of effective communication we've just discussed.

CHAPTER 3
BUILDING AND MAINTAINING RELATIONSHIPS

Navigating the intricacies of building and nurturing relationships can often feel like piecing together a complex jigsaw puzzle, especially when equipped with a unique set of pieces. Whether striking up a casual conversation, deepening a friendship, or fostering a romantic connection, each interaction holds the potential for enrichment and growth. This chapter is dedicated to enhancing your conversational skills, a fundamental aspect of relationship-building that can sometimes pose challenges for those on the autism spectrum. Here, you'll discover practical strategies to initiate and maintain engaging dialogues, ensuring that each conversation you embark on enriches your relationship landscape.

STARTING CONVERSATIONS: PRACTICAL TIPS AND SCRIPTS

Ice Breakers and Openers

Starting a conversation doesn't have to feel overwhelming. With the right tools, you can approach these situations with confidence and ease. Consider your context, as it's pivotal in selecting an appropriate conversation starter. At a social event, you might open with a light, context-related question like, "How do you know the host?" In a workplace setting, something as simple as commenting on a shared experience, such as a recent meeting or company event, can break the ice. "What did you think of today's presentation?" These openers serve as gentle nudges into conversation, setting a friendly tone and showing genuine interest in the other person's perspective.

When using these openers, it's essential to gauge the response and let the flow of dialogue lead the way. A warm, engaged reply is your cue to continue, while a short, unenthusiastic response might indicate it's best to end the exchange or shift the topic graciously. Paying attention to the person's tone and body language will significantly help in these situations.

Reading the Room

Assessing the social environment is crucial for choosing the right moment to initiate a conversation and the appropriate topics. Observing body language and listening to the tone of ongoing discussions can provide insights into the mood and openness of potential conversational partners. For instance, if you notice a group laughing and leaning in toward each other, it's likely a good moment to join in with a lighthearted comment. Conversely, closed-off body language, such as crossed arms and minimal eye contact, might suggest waiting for another opportunity is better.

Being attuned to these social cues allows you to navigate the social landscape more effectively, ensuring that your attempts at conversation are well-received and that you contribute positively to the group's dynamic.

Using Scripts Wisely

While having scripted lines can be incredibly helpful, especially in reducing anxiety about initiating conversations, it's crucial to use these scripts flexibly. Scripts should act as a safety net rather than a rigid guideline. For example, you might have a go-to script for meeting someone new, such as, "Hi, I'm [Your Name]. I noticed you were discussing [Topic]. I'm interested in that, too." This provides a structured way to enter a conversation, but it's important to adapt based on the response you receive. If the person shows interest, you can continue by asking a follow-up question; if they seem distracted or disinterested, it might be a cue to offer a polite closure to the exchange.

Practicing Small Talk

Engaging in small talk is a skill that can be developed through practice. Start small: Try commenting briefly about benign, everyday observations to a cashier or a coworker. For instance, a comment about the weather, "Beautiful sunny day, isn't it?" or a lighthearted remark about a typical situation, "Mondays always need a second cup of coffee, don't they?" can serve as practice. Over time, these interactions build confidence and reduce anxiety about initiating longer or more personal conversations.

Interactive Element: Role-Playing Exercise

To further enhance your conversation skills, engage in a role-playing exercise with a friend or a family member. Set up a scenario, such as a networking event or a party. Practice using different openers and reading responses. This safe, controlled environment allows you to experiment with various approaches and receive feedback, helping you refine your conversational skills in a supportive setting.

Mastering the art of starting conversations sets the stage for meaningful interactions that lead to lasting relationships. Whether these conversations blossom into friendships, professional connections, or romantic partnerships, each dialogue you engage in weaves a richer, more vibrant social tape. Embrace each opportunity to converse as a step toward building a fulfilling network of relationships, one conversation at a time.

MAINTAINING FRIENDSHIPS: UNDERSTANDING RECIPROCITY

Navigating the ebb and flow of friendships involves more than just spending time together; it requires a delicate balance of give and take. Friendship reciprocity is the mutual exchange of emotions, support, and resources, fostering an equitable and fulfilling relationship for all parties involved. Think of it as a dance where both partners lead and follow, ensuring that neither feels overburdened or underappreciated. Understanding and practicing this balance is crucial for sustaining healthy, long-lasting friendships.

Consider the scenario where you're always lending an ear or offering support, but when you need someone to listen to your concerns, your friends seem less available. Over time, this imbalance can lead to feelings of resentment or loneliness. To maintain reciprocity, openly discuss your needs and expectations with your friends. This doesn't mean keeping a scorecard of every interaction but instead fostering an environment where both parties feel comfortable expressing their needs and confident that they will be met with understanding and support. Additionally, actively seek opportunities to support your friends in ways that are meaningful to them. This could be anything from helping with a stressful move to sending a thoughtful message during tough times. By consciously engaging in these reciprocal actions, you reinforce the foundation of mutual support that characterizes strong friendships.

Recognizing and Setting Boundaries

While maintaining open lines of communication and support is essential, establishing and respecting personal boundaries is equally important. Boundaries help protect your emotional and physical well-being and are fundamental to any healthy relationship. They might range from needing time alone after a busy week to opting out of discussions on topics that trigger stress or discomfort. The key to setting effective boundaries lies in clear and compassionate communication. Start by reflecting on the necessary boundaries for your emotional and mental health. Once you have a clear understanding, communicate these boundaries to your friends in a straightforward yet respectful manner.

For instance, if you have a friend who often calls late at night to chat, disrupting your sleep, you might say, "I enjoy our conversations, but I need to stop taking calls after 10 p.m. so I can wind down and get a good night's sleep. Can we schedule our chats a bit earlier?" It's important to remember that setting boundaries is not about creating distance but maintaining a friendship where both parties feel respected and valued. By asserting your needs in a respectful manner, you are taking control of your relationships and ensuring that they are healthy and beneficial for both parties.

Activity-Based Friendships

Shared activities can significantly strengthen the bonds of friendship by creating common ground and shared memories. Whether joining a book club, enrolling in a cooking class, or participating in a local sports league, these activities can provide regular opportunities to connect and deepen your relationship. The memories you create together, the challenges you overcome, and the fun you have can all contribute to a more profound and enduring friendship.

When choosing activities, consider those that align with your and your friends' interests. This ensures that the experiences are enjoyable and engaging for everyone involved. If you're unsure what activities might be best, try exploring new hobbies together. This not only diversifies your experiences but also puts you both in the position of learners, which can make the activities more fun and less pressured. Over time, these shared interests and experiences can become the glue that holds your friendship together, even as other aspects of your lives change.

Handling Changes in Friendships

Friendships, like all relationships, evolve over time. Changes such as geographical moves, shifts in life stages, and developing personal interests can all impact the dynamics of a friendship. However, acknowledging and modifying these changes is not a sign of weakness but a testament to the adaptability and resilience of your relationship. For example, if a friend moves to a different city, think about how you can keep your connection. Regular video calls, planning visits, or maintaining an ongoing text or email conversation can help bridge physical distance, showing that your friendship can withstand any change.

Adapting to changes also means being open to the evolving nature of your interactions. Perhaps you used to meet for a weekly movie night, but now, with changes in schedules or locations, you might switch to a monthly dinner catch-up or a quarterly weekend getaway. Keeping the lines of communication open about these changes and being flexible and supportive of each other's evolving needs can help ensure that friendship continues to thrive in the face of life's inevitable shifts. Embracing these changes as opportunities to grow and learn more about each other and your friendship can continue to be a source of support and joy in both your lives.

ROMANTIC RELATIONSHIPS: FINDING AND SUSTAINING LOVE

Navigating romantic relationships can be deeply rewarding, yet it often requires a keen understanding of your emotional landscape and your partner's. Recognizing and addressing each other's emotional needs lays the groundwork for a connection, fostering a bond built on mutual understanding and deep empathy. It's more than just enjoying each other's company; it provides a supportive space where both partners feel seen, heard, and valued.

To get to this level of understanding, start by engaging in open conversations about your feelings, desires, and fears. This might feel uncomfortable, mainly if you're not accustomed to articulating your emotions. However, creating a habit of sharing your emotional states can significantly enhance the intimacy between you and your partner. For instance, if you're feeling overwhelmed by sensory inputs after a busy day, communicating this to your partner helps them understand your need for quiet time rather than leaving them guessing about your withdrawn mood. Similarly, encourage your partner to share their emotional needs. This mutual exchange helps you navigate day-to-day interactions more smoothly and deepens your emotional connection, making your relationship more resilient to stress and conflict.

Communication in Romance

Effective communication is the foundation of any thriving relationship. In romantic settings, this involves more than just sharing plans and coordinating schedules; it's about expressing affection and gratitude and resolving differences that strengthen the relationship. Start by incorporating affirmations into your daily interactions—a simple "I love how thoughtful you are" or "Thank you for being so understanding" can significantly impact your partner's sense of appreciation and worth. These expressions of gratitude and affection create a stronger bond between partners.

When discussing challenges or conflicts, approach these conversations with calmness and clarity. Avoid bringing up sensitive topics during a heated moment or when distracted. Instead, choose a quiet, private time when both of you are relaxed. Begin the conversation with affirmations and factual statements rather than accusations. For example, saying, "I feel hurt when interrupted because my opinions aren't valued," is more constructive than saying, "You never listen to me." By focusing on your feelings and needs without casting blame, you open a space for empathetic understanding and collaborative problem-solving.

Navigating Intimacy

Emotional and physical intimacy are vital aspects of any romantic relationship, but they are not without their complexities. It encompasses various interactions, from holding hands and cuddling to deeper physical connections. What's crucial is ensuring that both partners feel comfortable and consent to the forms of intimacy shared. Consent should be clear, enthusiastic, ongoing, checked, and reaffirmed as your relationship grows and evolves.

Understanding each other's comfort levels involves open, honest discussions where both partners feel safe expressing their boundaries and desires. For example, if you have specific sensitivities that affect physical touch, clearly communicate these to your partner, explaining what is enjoyable and uncomfortable for you. Likewise, invite your partner to share their preferences and limits. This mutual understanding enhances your physical connection and respects each individual's boundaries, reinforcing trust and respect in the relationship.

Long-Term Relationship Maintenance

Maintaining a long-term relationship requires intentional effort and commitment to keep the connection vibrant and engaging. Regular check-ins can be a valuable tool, providing a dedicated time to discuss your relationship's health, celebrate achievements, and address any concerns. These check-ins don't have to be formal; a simple conversation during a walk or over a cup of coffee can suffice. What's important is that both partners feel heard and that proactive steps are taken to nurture the relationship.

Incorporating regular date nights or special activities that both partners enjoy can keep the relationship exciting and dynamic. Whether trying out a new hobby together, planning a weekend getaway, or setting aside an evening to watch a favorite movie, these moments can significantly strengthen your bond. Additionally, setting mutual goals can give you something to strive toward together, whether related to fitness, travel, home improvement, or personal growth. Achieving these together creates shared memories and deepens your sense of teamwork and partnership.

Navigating romantic relationships with mindfulness and intention opens a world of mutual growth, support, and affection. By understanding and addressing emotional needs, communicating effectively, respecting intimacy boundaries, and actively maintaining the relationship, you lay the foundations for a partnership that survives and thrives in the face of life's challenges. As you continue to explore and strengthen these aspects, your relationship can become a source of profound joy and fulfillment, enriching your lives in unimaginable ways.

NETWORKING: BUILDING PROFESSIONAL RELATIONSHIPS

In the realm of professional growth, networking cannot be underestimated. It's about more than just exchanging business cards or adding contacts to your LinkedIn profile; it involves cultivating meaningful relationships that can open doors to new opportunities and support your career development. Understanding the nuances of professional etiquette is the cornerstone of effective networking. It begins with mastering the basics, such as making proper introductions. When you meet someone, offer a firm handshake and a warm smile, and introduce yourself clearly, stating your name and briefly what you do. This sets a professional tone and opens the dialogue for further conversation. Follow-up communications are equally essential. After meeting someone at a networking event or through a mutual connection, sending a timely, polite email acknowledging the meeting can reinforce the positive impression you made. Mention a detail from your conversation to personalize the message and express genuine interest in keeping the connection active.

Respectful interactions are the glue that holds professional relationships together. Always address people courteously, using their preferred titles or names, and listen attentively when they speak. Doing this shows respect and helps you better understand their interests and professional positions, enabling you to engage more thoughtfully. Remember, every interaction is an opportunity to demonstrate your professionalism and commitment to building respectful and mutually beneficial relationships.

Leveraging social media platforms, particularly LinkedIn, is a powerful strategy for expanding your professional network. Create a robust LinkedIn profile showcasing your skills, experiences, and professional interests. This serves as your digital portfolio that potential employers or collaborators can explore. Engaging with content on the platform is also crucial. Like, comment, and share posts that resonate with your professional interests, and don't hesitate to post your insights and experiences. This helps to increase your visibility and positions you as an active participant in your field. Reaching out to industry peers requires a tactful approach—constantly personalize your connection requests with a brief message explaining why you're interested in connecting, perhaps citing a shared interest or mutual connection. Giving this personal touch can make a notable difference in the response you receive.

Attending networking events is another essential aspect of building your professional network. Preparation is key—before the event, set clear objectives for what you hope to achieve, such as meeting potential mentors or learning about new developments in your field. Prepare a short self-introduction that succinctly summarizes who you are and what you do, making it easier to engage with new contacts. During the event, be proactive in starting conversations, using the skills discussed earlier for making introductions and small talk. Following up after the event is crucial; reach out to the people you met with personalized messages or emails, expressing your appreciation for the conversation and suggesting ways to collaborate or stay in touch.

Building a professional support network is invaluable for career growth and personal development. This network should include mentors who can offer guidance and advice, peers for mutual support, and even mentees, allowing you to give back and consolidate your knowledge. Identifying potential mentors can start with observing leaders in your field whose careers inspire you. Reach out with specific questions or requests for advice rather than a vague invitation to connect. Peers can be met through professional associations, conferences, or even LinkedIn groups. Engage regularly and genuinely with your network; share resources, provide support during challenges, and celebrate each other's successes. Over time, these relationships can offer career opportunities and a rich source of guidance, inspiration, and friendship.

Building and maintaining a robust professional network requires consistent effort and a genuine interest in mutual growth. You can significantly enhance your professional journey by adhering to professional etiquette, effectively leveraging digital platforms, actively participating in networking events, and nurturing a diverse support network. Each interaction is a step toward expanding your horizons, learning from others, and contributing to your field, making networking an essential skill in your professional toolkit.

DEALING WITH CONFLICT-EFFECTIVE RESOLUTION STRATEGIES

Navigating conflicts gracefully is a vital skill, mainly when cultivating lasting relationships, whether they are personal or professional. Conflict is a natural part of human interaction, arising from differences in viewpoints, desires, or expectations. Understanding the roots of these conflicts and adopting effective communication strategies can transform potential disputes into opportunities for growth and understanding.

Identifying Sources of Conflict

Conflicts can sprout from various sources, often intertwined with emotional undercurrents or unmet needs. Recognizing these sources is the first step toward resolution. For instance, miscommunication is a common source of conflict, where what was intended is not understood. Other times, conflicts arise from conflicting needs, such as when one person's desire for closeness clashes with another's need for space. Situational stressors, such as financial strain or work-related pressures, can also fuel conflicts, as they may reduce individuals' capacity for patience and magnify irritations. By pinpointing the actual root of the conflict, you can address the underlying issues more effectively than just the symptoms. Using this approach resolves the immediate dispute and the likelihood of similar conflicts arising in the future.

It's helpful to take a step back and analyze the situation calmly to identify these roots. Ask yourself what the real issue is, what each party wants, and why they want it. This kind of inquiry requires honest self-reflection and, often, open dialogue with the other party involved. It's about digging deeper than the surface arguments and uncovering the core of the disagreement, usually wrapped in emotional or relational needs.

Communication Techniques in Conflict

Once the root of a conflict is identified, effective communication is key to resolving it. The cornerstone of such communication is active listening, which involves truly hearing and trying to understand the other person's perspective without immediately planning your rebuttal. This shows respect for their feelings and viewpoints, which can help de-escalate tension. Another vital technique is using nonconfrontational language. Phrases like I understand your point, but I feel differently are less likely to provoke defensiveness than direct contradictions or criticisms. Additionally, focusing discussions on solutions rather than problems helps keep the conversation moving and constructive. Instead of dwelling on what went wrong, discuss how both parties can work together to improve the situation. This shift in focus can turn a conflict into a collaborative problem-solving session, reinforcing the relationship rather than straining it.

Role-Playing Conflict Scenarios

Practicing handling conflicts can significantly boost your confidence and effectiveness in real life. Role-playing exercises are beneficial for this. They allow you to simulate potential conflict scenarios in a controlled environment, where you can experiment with different approaches and receive feedback. For example, you might role-play a scenario with a friend where you disagree on plans for a joint project. Try strategies such as expressing your feelings clearly, compromising, standing firm on crucial points, and observing what works best. These practice sessions can reveal valuable insights into your conflict resolution style and help you refine your approach.

Preventing Escalation

Sometimes, despite best efforts, conflicts can intensify. To prevent escalation, it's crucial to recognize when emotions are running high and take proactive steps to cool down. Taking a timeout can be effective; it allows everyone involved to step away from the heat of the moment, calm down, and regain perspective. This pause can prevent the kind of spur-of-the-moment reactions that often exacerbate conflicts. In situations where both parties struggle to find common ground, bringing in a neutral third party can help ease a more objective discussion and aid in finding a resolution. Focusing on mutual benefits rather than individual wins can change the mood of the dynamic from adversarial to cooperative. It's about finding solutions that satisfy everyone's core needs, which often requires flexibility and creativity from all involved.

By adopting these strategies, you equip yourself with the tools to handle conflicts constructively. Instead of dreading disputes, you can view them as opportunities to strengthen relationships, enhance understanding, and foster deeper connections. Each conflict navigated successfully builds trust and resilience, enriching your interactions and life.

This exploration of conflict resolution strategies underscores the importance of understanding, communication, and proactive management in maintaining healthy relationships. By identifying the roots of conflicts, employing effective communication techniques, practicing through role-playing, and preventing escalation, you are better prepared to turn potential relationship pitfalls into strengthening moments. This chapter ties into the broader theme of building and sustaining relationships by emphasizing that conflict, when managed well, is inevitable and essential for growth. As we transition into the next chapter, we will explore other facets of personal and interpersonal development, continuing to build on the foundation of skills that enhance our interactions and understanding of ourselves and others.

CHAPTER 4
DAILY LIVING SKILLS FOR INDEPENDENCE

Living independently can seem unnerving, especially when you're managing the complexities of adult autism. One of the most pivotal aspects of independence is financial management—a skill that fosters personal freedom and significantly reduces stress and anxiety about the future. In this chapter, we'll unpack the essentials of managing finances efficiently, from understanding basic financial concepts to utilizing modern tools that simplify money management. This aims to give you the knowledge and resources to confidently handle your finances, making your pathway to independence smoother and more secure.

BUDGETING BASICS: MANAGING FINANCES WITH EASE

Understanding Financial Basics

Let's start with the foundation—understanding the basic components of financial management—income, expenses, savings, and budgeting. Income refers to the money you receive, which could come from employment, benefits, or other sources like investments. You spend money on expenses, from necessities such as rent and groceries to personal spending like entertainment. Savings represent the portion of your income for future needs or emergencies. Understanding these elements is crucial in managing your finances effectively.

To make these concepts more tangible, imagine your finances as a water system. Income is the water flowing into a tank, expenses are the various pipes the water flows through, and savings are the reservoir you keep aside, ensuring you always have water when you need it most. Budgeting controls the flow of water, ensuring that not everything drains out and that there's enough reserve for times when the supply might be low.

Creating a Budget

Creating a budget is your strategy for managing this flow. It involves putting all sources of income and expected expenses and allocating funds to each need, including savings. To accommodate specific autism-related needs, such as sensory items or therapies, it's important to categorize these as essential expenses in your budget. This ensures you always have the funds for this essential support without compromising in other areas.

Start by tracking your expenses for a month to see where your money goes. You might use a simple spreadsheet or a notebook for this purpose. Once you have a clear picture, categorize your expenses as "needs" (essentials like rent, food, and healthcare) and "wants" (nonessential items you could go without if necessary). This distinction helps make informed decisions about where to cut back, ensuring that your finances are directed first and foremost toward supporting your well-being and independence.

Tools for Financial Management

In today's digital age, numerous tools and apps can simplify financial management, making it less overwhelming and more accessible. Apps like Mint or YNAB (You Need a Budget) can be beneficial. They allow you to link your accounts and automatically categorize your spending, making it easy to see where your money is going each month. Many of these apps also offer features like setting up budgeting goals, reminders for bill payments, and alerts when you're nearing your spending limit in a particular category. For autistic adults, these tools can be invaluable in maintaining routine and order in financial management, providing a clear, visual representation of your financial health.

Dealing with Financial Stress

Financial stress is a common concern, but managing it effectively can lead to a more peaceful and secure life. One key strategy is establishing an emergency fund—having money to cover unexpected expenses like medical bills or car repairs without disrupting your budget. Start small, perhaps setting aside a small percentage of your monthly income, and gradually build it up to cover several months of living expenses.

It's also important to know when and how to seek financial advice. Whether consulting with a financial advisor to discuss investment options or contacting a debt counselor if you struggle with debt, professional guidance can provide direction and help you make informed decisions that align with your long-term financial goals. Learning simple financial decision-making techniques—such as comparing prices before purchasing, using discounts, or buying in bulk—can help stretch your budget further.

By embracing these strategies, you can alleviate the stress associated with financial management, paving the way for a more stable and independent life. Whether you're just starting on your own or looking to improve your financial skills, the tools and knowledge outlined here can empower you to take control of your finances confidently. As you apply these principles, you'll find that managing money becomes less intimidating and more strategic in building the independent life you aspire to lead.

MEAL PREPARATION: SIMPLE, SENSORY-FRIENDLY RECIPES

When it comes to meal preparation, embracing your unique sensory preferences is not just about satisfying taste buds—crafting a sensory-friendly environment that turns cooking from a necessity into a pleasurable activity. For many individuals on the autism spectrum, certain textures or flavors can be exceptionally comforting or, conversely, distressing. Recognizing and adapting your cooking to these sensory needs can transform your experience with food, making mealtime a more enjoyable and stress-free part of your day.

Choosing the Right Ingredients

Navigating the grocery store aisles or scanning an online food delivery app can be overwhelming if you're unsure what ingredients best suit your sensory preferences. Start by identifying textures and tastes that you find appealing or aversive. For example, if you find the texture of chunky tomatoes in sauces unsettling, consider smooth options or puree your tomatoes before adding them to dishes. On the flavor front, if you are sensitive to bitter tastes, you might steer clear of certain greens or excessively dark chocolate. Instead, opt for milder, sweeter vegetables like carrots and bell peppers or milk chocolate as an alternative.

When shopping, take your time to explore different brands and products that might better meet your sensory needs. Many stores offer samples or return policies, allowing you to try products without committing to a complete purchase. Additionally, reading online reviews can provide insights into the sensory aspects of products from individuals who may share similar preferences. This proactive approach ensures that the ingredients you choose are comforting and helps expand your culinary repertoire in a way that respects your sensory preferences.

Simple Cooking Techniques

Mastering a few basic cooking techniques can significantly enhance your ability to prepare meals that cater to your sensory needs. For example, steaming vegetables rather than frying or boiling can preserve their mild flavors and offer a softer texture. Learning to sauté or roast vegetables with olive oil can provide a satisfying crunch without deep-frying if you prefer crispy textures.

Focusing on one-pot meals can be a game-changer for those new to cooking or who find following complex recipes challenging. These meals require less preparation and minimal cooking skills, reducing kitchen-related stress. Slow or pressure cookers are excellent for this cooking style, allowing you to combine ingredients once all the ingredients are in the cooker, set the timer, and have a fully cooked meal. This method simplifies the cooking process and minimizes the sensory overload from managing multiple pots and pans on the stove.

Meal Planning Tips

Planning your meals is a strategic way to reduce stress and ensure your dietary needs are met throughout the week. Start by creating a meal schedule that outlines your plan for each meal. This doesn't have to be rigid; flexibility is key in accommodating last-minute changes in appetite or preferences. Along with the schedule, prepare a shopping list that aligns with your planned meals, which helps make grocery shopping more efficient and less overwhelming.

Preparing ingredients in advance can also streamline your cooking process. Dedicating a few hours each week to washing, chopping, and storing vegetables or precooking certain staples like rice or pasta can save time during busier days. Store these prepped ingredients in clear, labeled containers in the refrigerator, making them easy to grab when it's time to cook. This organization minimizes the time spent in the kitchen and reduces the sensory demands of meal preparation, making the process smoother and more enjoyable.

Adapting Recipes for Sensory Needs

Adapting recipes to better suit your sensory needs can be creative and fulfilling. If a recipe calls for an ingredient or texture you find uncomfortable, don't hesitate to substitute it with something more palatable. For instance, if a salad recipe includes raw onions that you find too intense, try soaking the chopped onions in water before adding them to the salad to reduce their intensity, or substitute with a milder vegetable like cucumbers.

Experimenting with cooking methods can also alter textures to suit your preferences. For example, cooking vegetables, braising, or stewing can achieve the desired consistency if you prefer softer textures. Conversely, for those who enjoy crispier textures, grilling or broiling can add a delightful crunch to your meals.

Through these adaptations, meal preparation becomes about sustenance, personalization, and comfort, turning the kitchen into a sanctuary where your sensory preferences are accommodated and celebrated. Whether it's modifying ingredients, tweaking cooking techniques, or strategically planning your meals, these strategies ensure that each dining experience is tailored to your unique sensory profile, enhancing your independence and enjoyment of food.

ORGANIZING YOUR LIVING SPACE FOR SENSORY COMFORT

Creating a comfortable living space that supports your sensory needs can transform your home into a sanctuary where stress and sensory overload are minimized. Understanding and catering to your unique sensory preferences is the first step in this process. This might involve assessing how various sensory inputs, such as light, sound, and texture, affect you throughout the day. For instance, you might find that natural light uplifts your mood or that certain fabric textures feel more soothing against your skin. Taking note of these preferences helps make informed decisions about setting up and maintaining your living environment.

When organizing your living space, the principle of "less is more" often holds, especially if clutter exacerbates your stress or sensory overload. Start by decluttering your space, which doesn't just mean disposing of unwanted items but also organizing what you decide to keep so that everything has a designated place. Reducing visual clutter makes it easier to locate items when needed, reducing anxiety and saving time. Choosing the proper lighting can also significantly impact your sensory comfort. If you're sensitive to bright light, try softer, dimmable lighting options that allow you to adjust the brightness. When arranging furniture, consider creating distinct zones that cater to different activities—such as a quiet reading nook with a comfy chair away from high-traffic areas or a designated workspace with minimal distractions. This helps reduce sensory overlap and allows better control over your environment according to your activities.

Incorporating sensory tools effectively in your living space can greatly enhance your comfort level. Noise-canceling headphones can be a sanctuary for your ears in a noisy environment, allowing you to enjoy peace and quiet or listen to calming sounds without external disturbances. Weighted blankets can offer a comforting, grounding presence during rest or moments of sensory overload, providing gentle pressure that mimics the feeling of being held. Scent diffusers, candles, or incense can also create a calming ambiance; choosing scents that you find comforting can help reduce anxiety and promote relaxation. Place these tools strategically around your home where you can easily access them, especially in areas where you spend most of your time or where you're most likely to experience sensory overload.

Maintaining a sensory-friendly environment is an ongoing process that requires regular attention. Establishing a cleaning schedule that suits your sensory and energy levels helps keep your space tidy without becoming overwhelming. For instance, instead of cleaning in one day, you might spread tasks throughout the week—vacuuming on one day, dusting on another, and so on. This keeps your space pleasant and prevents the buildup of sensory irritants like dust and clutter. Be mindful of how your sensory needs may change over time. Regularly reassessing and adjusting your environment to accommodate these changes is key. For example, you might find that you become more sensitive to light or sound as you age or that your preferences for certain textures change. Updating your space to reflect these evolving needs ensures that your home continues to provide comfort and support.

By assessing, organizing, and maintaining your living space with a focus on sensory comfort, you create an environment that meets your practical needs and supports your well-being. This tailored approach allows you to thrive in your own space, making your home a true personal retreat where you can relax, recharge, and enjoy life with minimal sensory stress.

TIME MANAGEMENT TOOLS AND TECHNIQUES

Understanding time management is not just about keeping to a schedule or checking off tasks; it's a fundamental skill that enhances your independence and reduces stress and anxiety in your daily life. When you manage your time effectively, you're ensuring that essential tasks are completed and allowing you to relax, pursue interests, and engage socially in critical aspects of a balanced and fulfilling life. For individuals with autism who might experience heightened anxiety or stress from unexpected changes or unstructured time, mastering time management can be remarkably empowering.

Let's break down time management into its core components. Effective time management involves anticipating, planning, and designating time for tasks according to their importance and urgency. This might sound straightforward, but when sensory processing or executive functioning challenges are part of your daily experience, it can become a complex puzzle. For instance, a seemingly simple task like preparing for an appointment involves multiple steps—choosing clothes, traveling, managing social interactions, and processing sensory inputs—all must be planned and timed carefully to ensure a smooth and stress-free experience.

To start, consider using planners and calendars—tools that can significantly enhance your ability to manage time. Digital calendars, like Google Calendar, offer the advantage of setting up reminders that can alert you at multiple intervals (a day before, an hour before, etc.), ensuring you're well-prepared for upcoming events or tasks. These tools are handy for visual thinkers, as they allow you to see your week or month at a glance, color-code different types of activities, and easily adjust plans as needed. For those who prefer something tangible, a physical planner can serve a similar purpose, with the added benefit of tactile engagement in writing down and checking off tasks, which can be satisfying and grounding.

Prioritizing tasks is a skill that can dramatically enhance efficiency and reduce feeling overwhelmed. You identify the urgent and essential tasks and tackle these first. If delayed, this might include appointments, deadlines, or functions with significant consequences. Next, look at important but not urgent tasks, such as regular exercise or pursuing a hobby, that contribute to your long-term well-being. Learning to recognize and adjust priorities based on unexpected events is also crucial. For example, if you suddenly need to visit a doctor, being able to shift your schedule around without significant stress is a testament to good time management. Tools like the Eisenhower Box can help make these decisions more straightforward, categorizing tasks into four quadrants based on urgency and importance, simplifying the decision-making process.

Building routine and structure into your daily life can provide comfort and predictability, which is especially beneficial for autistic adults. Routines reduce the cognitive load of planning every day from scratch, providing a framework within which spontaneity can occur in a controlled manner. Gradually building these routines—anchoring events like meals and bedtime—can help form a stable pattern. Over time, these routines become second nature, reducing anxiety around "what comes next" and freeing up mental energy for more enjoyable or challenging tasks.

Adapting routines as needed is part of life's natural ebb and flow. Being flexible enough to adjust your routines in response to life changes—such as a new job, a move, or changing health needs—is as important as establishing them in the first place. Regularly reassess your routines to ensure they still serve your needs effectively. This might mean changing your exercise schedule, shifting your work hours, or finding new ways to relax and unwind. Remember, the goal of time management is not to regiment every moment of your day but to create a flexible structure that maximizes your productivity and personal satisfaction.

By embracing these time management strategies and tools, you can enhance your ability to navigate daily life with greater ease and confidence. Whether using digital tools to keep track of appointments, prioritizing tasks to focus on what truly matters, or establishing routines that provide stability and structure, the skills you develop in time management are invaluable assets in your journey toward independence and well-being.

PERSONAL CARE ROUTINES FOR HEALTH AND HYGIENE

Personal care involves much more than just keeping clean; it's about creating routines that maintain your hygiene and respect your sensory sensitivities, enhancing your physical and social well-being. Effective personal care routines can significantly impact how you feel about yourself and interact with others, making them essential components of your daily life.

Basic Hygiene Practices

Understanding and implementing basic hygiene practices such as bathing, dental care, and grooming are fundamental. Regular bathing helps remove dirt and oils, preventing skin irritations and infections, and fosters refreshment. Dental care, including brushing and flossing, protects against oral diseases and ensures fresh breath, which is crucial for close interactions. Grooming, which may involve shaving, hair care, and nail care, affects your appearance and influences how others perceive and interact with you in social or professional settings. These practices are pivotal in maintaining your health and boosting your confidence, making them indispensable parts of your daily routine.

Creating a personal care routine that accommodates your sensory needs can transform these necessary tasks into enjoyable experiences. For instance, if you find certain scents or the feeling of grooming tools uncomfortable, opting for unscented products or noninvasive tools can make a significant difference. Look for toiletries specified as "for sensitive skin" or hypoallergenic, which are less likely to cause irritation. When selecting tools, such as toothbrushes or combs, consider those with softer bristles or wider-toothed combs, which can be gentler on your skin and scalp.

Dealing with Sensory Issues in Personal Care

Sensory issues often manifest prominently in personal care routines. Adjustments to how you perform these tasks can mitigate discomfort and transform your care routine into a soothing ritual. If you are sensitive to water temperature, experimenting with different temperatures can help you find a comfortable setting, making bathing a relaxing rather than stressful experience. For those who find hair brushing painful, detangling sprays or brushes designed to minimize pulling can reduce discomfort. Similarly, clothing textures play a crucial role in your daily comfort. Opting for garments made from soft, natural fibers without restrictive bands can enhance your physical comfort throughout the day.

Adapting your environment to suit your sensory preferences is also crucial. For example, using softer lighting in your bathroom can make grooming more pleasant if you are sensitive to bright lights. Playing calming music or sounds during your care routines can also help mask less pleasant sensory inputs, such as the sound of a hairdryer or the feel of a razor, making these necessary tasks more bearable and enjoyable.

Health Monitoring and Maintenance

Regular health check-ups are vital in catching potential issues early and managing ongoing conditions, including those related to sensory sensitivities. Regularly visiting healthcare providers for regular assessments can ensure your physical health is monitored and maintained. Additionally, learning how to monitor your health at home, such as checking your blood pressure or managing dietary needs, empowers you to take proactive steps toward your well-being.

Maintaining a relationship with healthcare providers who understand and respect your sensory needs can significantly enhance the quality of care you receive. It's important to communicate openly with your doctors or therapists about your sensitivities so they can adjust their methods or the environment accordingly. For instance, a dentist can minimize your time in the waiting room or use quieter tools to reduce sensory overload during appointments.

By integrating these strategies into your personal care routines, you ensure that your hygiene and health are maintained and create a daily routine that respects and accommodates your unique sensory profile. This tailored approach enhances your physical well-being and boosts your confidence and independence, making personal care a rewarding part of your daily life.

As we conclude this chapter on daily living skills for independence, we've explored essential aspects that enhance your ability to manage finances, prepare meals, organize your living space, manage time, and take care of your hygiene—all crucial for a fulfilling and autonomous life. Each skill we've developed is a step toward greater independence and confidence, allowing you to navigate the complexities of life with assurance and ease. As we move forward, remember that each small step in mastering these skills contributes to a larger picture of personal success and satisfaction.

Imagine a world where autism is not a barrier but a gateway to profound self-awareness, a life of improved communication, and the attainment of emotional balance.

You are not alone. Here's your chance to redefine your experiences in a world that often fails to understand honesty.

To make that happen, I have a question for you ...

Would you help someone you've never met, even if you never got credit for it?

Who is this person you ask? They are like you. Or, at least, like you used to be. Less experienced, wanting to make a difference, and needing help but unsure where to look.

My mission is to make this Autism Support Guide accessible to everyone. Everything I do stems from that mission. And the only way to accomplish that mission is by reaching ... well ... everyone.

This is where you come in. Most people do, in fact, judge a book by its cover (and its reviews). So here's my ask on behalf of a struggling autistic adult, a parent struggling to understand, or a professional working with adults on the spectrum you've never met.

Please help these people attain the information they need to live successful, enriching lives by leaving a review.

Your gift costs no money and takes less than 60 seconds, but it can change a fellow autistic person's life forever. Your review could help ...

- ... one small business employ someone on the spectrum in their community.
- ... one more parent support their family more effectively.
- ... one more client transforms their life.
- ... one more dream come true.

To get that "feel good" feeling and help this person for real, all you have to do is ... and it takes less than 60 seconds.

Leave a review.

Simply scan the QR code to leave your review:

If you feel good about helping a faceless autistic adult, you are my kind of person. Welcome to the club. You are one of us.

I'm much more excited than you can possibly imagine to help you achieve your desired outcomes by incorporating what you learn from reading this book. You'll love the strategies and lessons I share in the coming chapters.

Thank you from the bottom of my heart. Now, back to our regularly scheduled program.

   - Your biggest fan, L. Celeste

PS: **Fun fact**: If you provide something of value to another person, it makes you more valuable to them. If you'd like goodwill straight from another person dealing with autism and you believe this book will help them, send this book their way.

CHAPTER 5
NAVIGATING THE SENSORY WORLD

Creating a sensory-friendly home is more than comfort—designing a living space that respects your sensory experiences, allowing you to thrive in your sanctuary. Whether it's the color of the walls, the lighting, or the furniture arrangement, each element plays a crucial role in how you interact with your environment. For those with sensory sensitivities, these choices can be the difference between a place that feels like a haven and one that perpetuates stress. Let's explore how you can tailor your living space to meet your sensory needs, enhancing your comfort and ability to engage with the world around you.

DESIGNING A SENSORY-FRIENDLY HOME

Assessing Home Environment Needs

First, consider the sensory inputs that most significantly affect you. Is it noise, light, texture, or color? Or perhaps spatial arrangements and the flow of movement within your rooms? Understanding your sensitivities is key to making informed decisions about your living environment. Start by walking through your space, noting any areas that consistently make you feel uncomfortable or overwhelmed. It might be a brightly lit kitchen that intensifies your light sensitivity or a cluttered hallway that hinders your movement and impacts your mood.

Once you've identified these areas, consider the changes that could mitigate discomfort. For instance, if fluorescent lights in your kitchen are too harsh, could they be replaced with adjustable LED lights? What storage solutions could help maintain a more apparent living space if clutter is an issue? Assessing your environment through this approach allows you to prioritize modifications that will significantly impact your daily comfort and functionality.

Use of Color and Lighting

The colors and lighting in your home can profoundly influence your sensory satisfaction. Too bright or overly stimulating colors might cause discomfort, while an environment that is too dim could lead to strain and fatigue. Opt for hues that bring you a sense of calm and relaxation. Soft, muted colors like pastel blues, greens, and warm earth tones often create a serene atmosphere. You might consider using color psychology as a guide to choose shades that evoke the feelings you wish to cultivate in your home.

Lighting, similarly, should be adaptable to your needs. Natural light is wonderfully beneficial for many, but its intensity needs to be manageable. Light-filtering curtains are a great option, allowing you to soften bright daylight without darkening your space too much. For artificial lighting, choose options that mimic natural light and use dimmers that will enable you to adjust the brightness when needed. This control can significantly reduce the likelihood of sensory overload and create an environment that adapts to sensory input needs.

Furniture and Layout

Selecting and arranging the right furniture thoughtfully can significantly enhance your sensory environment. Choose pieces that feel good to the touch and do not overwhelm your space. Soft, rounded furniture minimizes the risk of injury and contributes to a gentle, welcoming atmosphere. Avoid overly bulky items that can make a space feel cramped, and opt for more streamlined, functional pieces.

When arranging your furniture, aim for a layout that allows easy movement. Ensure there are clear pathways between rooms and within common areas. This helps reduce physical obstacles and makes the space visually simpler and less likely to trigger sensory discomfort. Consider the functionality of each room—grouping furniture in a way that promotes efficient and enjoyable use of the space. For example, in your living room, a cozy reading nook with a soft armchair, adequate lighting, and a nearby bookshelf create a designated area for relaxation without cluttering the central part of the room.

Incorporating Sensory Zones

Creating specific areas within your home dedicated to sensory relaxation can provide safe spots for decompression and enjoyment. A quiet corner of your living room outfitted with a comfortable seat, some plush pillows, and perhaps a throw blanket can serve as a perfect retreat when you need to escape from the sensory demands of daily life. Soft lighting, calming wall colors, and the absence of electronic distractions can enhance this area's soothing properties.

Those benefiting from sensory engagement should consider setting up a sensory play area. This space could include tactile mats, a small sandbox, or auditory toys like rainmakers or soft musical instruments. Tailoring this area to include sensory input that you find pleasant or stimulating can provide a therapeutic outlet within your home.

Textual Element: Sensory-Friendly Home Checklist

- Assess each room for potential sensory triggers.
- Create adjustable lighting solutions with dimmers or customizable LED systems.
- Choose wall colors in muted, soothing tones.
- Select furniture that is soft, rounded, and proportionate to your space.
- Designate specific areas for relaxation and sensory engagement.
- Implement storage solutions to reduce clutter and maintain clear pathways.

By thoughtfully assessing and modifying your living environment to address your sensory needs, you transform your home into a supportive space that meets your functional needs and respects and nurtures your sensory preferences. This proactive approach to designing a sensory-friendly home empowers you to engage with your environment on your terms, enhancing your comfort and overall well-being.

COPING MECHANISMS FOR PUBLIC PLACES

Navigating public spaces can sometimes feel taxing, especially if you're sensitive to sensory inputs like noise, light, or crowds. However, with the proper preparation and tools, you can greatly reduce the stress and discomfort associated with these environments. Let's explore practical strategies to help you handle public spaces more quickly and confidently.

Preparation Strategies

Preparing for an outing involves more than just deciding where to go. It starts with understanding the sensory challenges you might face and planning how to mitigate them. Before visiting a new place, try to gather as much information as possible about the environment. Many venues now offer sensory-friendly sessions or quiet hours, which can provide a more comfortable experience. Websites and customer service lines can be invaluable resources for this information. Additionally, visiting during less busy times, such as weekday mornings, can help you avoid the peak crowds that often heighten sensory overload.

Bringing along sensory tools can also significantly improve your comfort. Noise-canceling headphones can mute overwhelming background noise, allowing you to focus more on your activities than the environment. Similarly, carrying tactile fidget tools can provide a soothing distraction during moments of stress. Packing these items might seem like a small step, but it can profoundly impact your ability to stay calm and enjoy your outing.

Navigating Crowded Spaces

Crowded environments are particularly challenging due to the unpredictable nature of human movement and noise. One effective way to manage this is through visualization techniques. Before entering a crowded space, take a few moments to visualize the layout and imagine yourself moving confidently through the area. This mental preparation can reduce anxiety and make you feel more in control once you are in the environment.

Once there, look for exits and quieter areas to take breaks if the sensory input becomes too intense. Many public spaces, such as malls or museums, have areas designated for rest or less traffic, which can provide temporary relief from the hustle and bustle. Setting time limits for exposure to crowded regions can also help manage energy and sensory input, allowing you to engage with the environment on your terms without becoming overwhelmed.

Using Technology Aids

Technology offers a range of aids to help you navigate public spaces more comfortably. Apps that provide real-time information about crowd sizes or noise levels in public venues can help you decide the best times and places to visit. Some apps are designed to alert you to areas with lower sensory inputs or navigate you through quieter routes.

Moreover, apps that produce soothing sounds or meditative music can be invaluable in masking background noise, helping you maintain a sense of calm in noisy environments. Utilizing these technological tools makes public outings more manageable and empowers you to manage your sensory environment proactively.

Self-Advocacy in Public

Advocating for your sensory needs in public spaces is crucial. It starts with communicating your needs clearly to those you're with, whether they're friends, family, or colleagues. Letting them know what you need to feel comfortable can help them support you in finding or creating a more suitable environment during outings.

It's also important to know your rights regarding accessibility. Many regions have laws and regulations that protect the rights of individuals with disabilities, including those related to sensory processing. Familiarizing yourself with these rights can empower you to request necessary accommodations, such as early flight boarding or access to quiet rooms in public venues. Whether seeking assistance from staff or using priority seating, knowing and asserting your rights can make a significant difference in your public experiences.

By employing these strategies, you equip yourself with the tools and confidence to navigate public spaces despite sensory challenges. Preparation, sensory tools, strategic use of technology, and effective self-advocacy are all steps that enhance your ability to engage with the world around you, turning what might once have been a source of significant stress into an opportunity for enjoyable exploration.

CHOOSING APPROPRIATE CLOTHING FOR SENSORY COMFORT

When it comes to dressing in comfort, not just any fabric or fit will do, especially when you are sensitive to how clothing feels on your skin. The textures, weights, and construction of your clothes can significantly impact your comfort and sensory experience throughout the day. Understanding the different types of fabrics and how they interact with your sensory preferences is crucial. Natural fibers like cotton and bamboo are typically recommended because they are breathable and gentle on the skin, reducing the chances of irritation. These materials also regulate temperature well, keeping you comfortable in various weather conditions. On the other hand, synthetic fibers, while sometimes necessary for durability or weather resistance, can be more likely to cause discomfort or overheating, so it's important to choose wisely based on your activities and needs.

The fit of your clothing also plays a significant role in your sensory comfort. Tight, restrictive garments might cause discomfort, while too loose clothes could become bothersome by moving around too much. Opting for clothing with a relaxed fit that still contours comfortably to your body can provide balance, ensuring comfort without adding unnecessary sensory input. Additionally, consider clothing with minimal seams and tags or even tag-free garments. For many, the sensation of a tag against the skin can be irritating; removing tags or choosing clothes designed without them can alleviate this issue.

Adapting your clothing to increase comfort doesn't have to be complicated. Simple modifications can make a significant difference. For example, if tags bother you, cutting them off carefully can eliminate discomfort. If you find seams irritating, look for garments labeled as seamless, which are increasingly available, especially in activewear. For those who dislike the tightness of traditional socks, opting for seamless versions or those designed without restrictive bands can enhance comfort. While seemingly minor, small changes can significantly improve how you feel in your clothes, making your day-to-day experiences more pleasant and less sensory-challenging.

Balancing sensory comfort with practicality and safety, especially in different environmental settings, is another aspect to consider when choosing clothing. If you spend a lot of time outdoors in the sun, lightweight, long-sleeved shirts can protect your skin from the sun while keeping you cool. Layering with soft, breathable fabrics in colder climates can help maintain body warmth without overwhelming your senses. Each setting might require different clothing strategies; understanding these needs can help you prepare better, ensuring comfort wherever you are.

Building a wardrobe that respects your sensory needs takes time and intention. Start by assessing your current collection, identifying pieces that meet your sensory and practical needs, and note what does not work for you. When shopping for new clothing, prioritize materials and fits you know are comfortable. It's often helpful to shop in stores where you can touch and feel the fabrics and try on garments before buying. However, online shopping can be a viable alternative if in-store shopping is overwhelming. Many online stores now offer detailed fabric information and customer reviews that can give you a sense of how a garment feels and fits before making a purchase. Remember, creating a sensory-friendly wardrobe is a personal and ongoing process. It's about making choices that enhance your comfort and well-being, allowing you to feel good inside and out.

Strategies for Reducing Visual and Auditory Overload

Understanding how to control visual and auditory stimuli is crucial when managing sensory overload. This isn't just about avoiding discomfort; it's about creating environments and habits that enhance one's ability to function and feel at ease in everyday situations. Let's explore practical ways to manage these sensory inputs, ensuring one can navigate one's day more comfortably and with less stress.

Controlling Visual Stimuli

Visual overload can occur in environments with excessive brightness, flickering lights, or intricate or vibrant patterns. One simple yet effective way to manage this is by using sunglasses or tinted lens glasses, which can significantly reduce the harshness of bright lights indoors under fluorescent lighting or outside on a sunny day. Consider the color schemes of your surroundings for indoor settings, particularly in your home or workspace. Decorating with soothing, monochromatic color schemes can help create a visually calming space. Soft blues, greens, or warm grays can reduce visual stimulation and make your environment more comfortable. Additionally, be mindful of lighting choices. Opt for lamps and fixtures that allow you to adjust brightness and use bulbs emitting soft, natural light to minimize glare and discomfort.

Another aspect to consider is the presence of screens and digital devices, which are integral to modern life but can be significant sources of visual strain. If your day involves substantial screen time, make use of features like blue light filters or screen dimmers that many devices now offer. These settings can help reduce eye strain and prevent fatigue from prolonged exposure to harsh screen light. It's also beneficial to arrange your workspace so that there is no direct glare at your screen and to take regular breaks, giving yourself a time limit. For example, every 30 minutes, look at something 20 feet away for at least 30 seconds to rest your eyes.

Managing Auditory Inputs

Auditory overload can be just as jarring as visual, particularly in environments with a cacophony of sounds, from traffic noise to overlapping conversations. Using earplugs or noise-canceling headphones can provide a barrier to unwanted sounds, allowing you to control your auditory environment effectively. These tools are handy in public spaces or workplaces with less control over ambient noise.

Creating routines that limit exposure to noisy environments can also play a crucial role in managing auditory sensitivity. Plan your activities during times when noise levels are typically lower. For example, shopping early in the morning or visiting cafés during their off-peak hours can result in a quieter, more manageable experience. At home, you can designate quiet times during which electronic devices are turned down or off and noisy household activities are minimized. This helps create a more serene environment and establish a routine that can make daily life predictable and less anxiety-inducing.

Techniques for Immediate Relief

Despite the best preparations, there might be times when sensory overload becomes overwhelming. Having techniques for immediate relief can be a lifesaver in such situations. Focused breathing is a powerful tool that can help calm the mind, reducing the intensity of sensory input. The practice of deep, slow breaths, inhaling through your nose and exhaling through your mouth, helps center your thoughts and lower your stress levels. Visualization techniques can also be effective; imagine yourself in a place that you find peaceful and serene, focusing on the details of this haven until you feel your anxiety lessen.

A predetermined quiet space, whether at home or in a familiar public place, can provide a crucial sanctuary when sensory inputs become too much. This space should be somewhere you can control the environment quickly, adjusting lighting, sound, and seating to ensure maximum comfort.

Long-Term Adaptation Strategies

Consider strategies like gradual exposure and cognitive behavioral techniques for long-term management of sensory sensitivity. Gradual exposure involves slowly and systematically exposing yourself to higher levels of sensory input, allowing your system to adjust over time. This should be done carefully and ideally under the guidance of a professional who can support you.

Cognitive behavioral strategies can also help you change how you perceive and react to sensory stimuli. Techniques such as cognitive reframing can help you alter negative thinking patterns about sensory experiences, potentially reducing the distress they cause. Regular mindfulness practices, such as meditation or tai chi, can enhance your ability to regulate your responses to sensory inputs, increasing your tolerance levels and overall sensory processing. Apps such as Aura, Soothing Pod, and Insight Timer are wonderful tools to help you accomplish this.

Using these strategies in your routine can enhance your ability to manage visual and auditory overload, making everyday environments more navigable and less stressful. Whether through immediate relief techniques or long-term adaptation strategies, the goal is to empower you to live more comfortably and fully, regardless of your sensory sensitivities.

CREATING A PERSONALIZED SENSORY DIET

Understanding and managing your unique sensory needs can significantly enhance your daily life, reducing stress and enabling you to engage more fully with the world around you. A concept that can be incredibly beneficial in this regard is a sensory diet. This term might suggest food, but it refers to a carefully planned series of physical activities and accommodations to help individuals maintain optimal sensory input. Think of it as nourishment for your senses, providing just the right amount of stimulation to keep you balanced and focused throughout the day.

A sensory diet is beneficial because everyone's sensory needs are different. What overstimulates one person might barely register for another. For example, while one person might find a loud party overwhelming, another might thrive in that bustling environment. Understanding your sensory profile is the first step in creating a diet that works for you. This can be done through self-assessment tools that help you track your reactions to various sensory inputs, or, ideally, with the help of a professional like an occupational therapist trained in sensory integration therapy. They can offer insights and guidance on effectively structuring your activities to meet your sensory needs.

Once you understand your sensory preferences and triggers, you can design a diet that fits your daily routine. This might include specific physical activities that provide the sensory input you need. For instance, if you benefit from deep pressure to feel grounded, your sensory diet might consist of time with a weighted blanket or wearing a weighted vest during certain parts of the day. If you're hypersensitive to sensory input, your diet might focus on activities that calm and reduce sensory overload, such as dimming lights, using noise-canceling headphones, or having access to a quiet space where you can retreat when you need to decompress.

Various sensory activities throughout your day can help keep your sensory system well-regulated. This might look like starting your morning with a few minutes of stretching or heavy muscle work like yoga, which can help to wake up your body. Throughout the day, scheduled breaks for activities that meet your sensory needs—like chewing gum if you need oral stimulation or taking a brisk walk if you need movement—can help maintain your equilibrium. The key is consistency and regularity, ensuring that these activities are spread throughout the day to meet your sensory needs continuously.

Regularly evaluating the effectiveness of your sensory diet is crucial. Over time, your sensory needs might change due to various factors like stress, aging, or changes in your environment or routine. Regular check-ins, where you assess whether your current sensory diet is meeting your needs or if it's causing sensory overload or understimulation, are essential. This might mean increasing or decreasing the intensity of the sensory input or introducing new activities while phasing out others that are no longer effective. Keeping a sensory diary can be helpful here, allowing you to note patterns and changes in your sensory experiences and adjust your diet accordingly.

You can effectively manage your sensory environment by understanding the concept of a sensory diet, identifying your personal sensory needs, designing a tailored plan, and regularly adjusting it. This proactive approach enhances your daily functioning and comfort and empowers you to engage with life more fully, embracing experiences with confidence and resilience.

CHAPTER 6
MENTAL HEALTH AND EMOTIONAL WELL-BEING

Navigating the landscape of mental health can sometimes feel like trying to find your way through a dense, unfamiliar forest. Just as each person's journey through a forest is unique—marked by their paths, obstacles, and discoveries—so, too, is each individual's experience with mental health, particularly for adults on the autism spectrum. In this chapter, we'll explore the often-subtle signs of anxiety and depression, offer strategies for monitoring your emotional state, and discuss the importance of seeking professional help when needed. Understanding and addressing these aspects can enhance your emotional well-being, paving the way for a more fulfilling and balanced life.

IDENTIFYING SYMPTOMS OF ANXIETY AND DEPRESSION

Recognizing Anxiety

Anxiety in autistic adults can manifest in ways that might not immediately be recognized by those unfamiliar with how autism intersects with mental health. Increased stimming behaviors—such as hand-flapping, rocking, or difficulty finding words, particularly during stress or uncertainty. These behaviors are often a coping mechanism to manage sensory overload or emotional distress. Additionally, you might find yourself avoiding situations you previously navigated without concern, from social gatherings to routine outings like grocery shopping. This avoidance can be a protective response, attempting to minimize scenarios that could escalate feelings of anxiety.

Disruptions in routine, which might seem minor to some, can also precipitate anxiety in autistic adults. The comfort of predictability is replaced with the stress of uncertainty, which can feel overwhelming. For instance, your sleeping patterns, appetite, or general mood may change during these times. Recognizing these signs is the first step in managing anxiety. By identifying what triggers these feelings and understanding how they manifest in your body, you can begin taking control of your reactions and making informed decisions about handling them.

Depression Indicators

Depression in autistic adults often goes beyond the typical markers of sadness or fatigue. It might manifest through a withdrawal from social interactions—even previously enjoyable ones. This isn't just about preferring solitude; it's a noticeable reduction in engaging with the world around you. You might also lose interest in activities that once brought joy, whether a favorite hobby, watching a beloved show, or reading. These changes can be gradual, making them hard to notice initially, but they can significantly impact your quality of life.

Another indicator of depression can be a change in your sleep patterns. This might mean sleeping significantly more than usual or experiencing insomnia. Changes in appetite, whether increased or decreased, can also signal that not all is well. These physical symptoms are often intertwined with emotional states and can serve as important indicators that your mental health may need attention.

Self-Monitoring Techniques

Maintaining a mood diary can be an invaluable tool for tracking your emotional state. This doesn't have to be a detailed journal; even a simple log of your daily moods, activities, and overall feelings can help you identify patterns and triggers in your emotional life. Apps designed to track mood and mental health can also be helpful, providing a structured way to monitor your well-being and offering reminders to check in with yourself throughout the day.

The act of tracking your mood not only helps in recognizing the early signs of anxiety and depression but also empowers you to take proactive steps toward managing your mental health. It can facilitate discussions with healthcare providers by providing concrete examples of your emotional experiences and their impacts on your daily life.

When to Seek Help

Recognizing when to seek help is crucial. If you find that symptoms of anxiety or depression persist despite your efforts to manage them, or if they begin to interfere significantly with your daily life, it may be time to reach out for professional support. Getting help early can prevent symptoms from worsening and can help you find ways to manage your mental health effectively.

Knowing how and when to seek help is essential. You can start by talking to a loved one or consulting with your primary healthcare provider, who can refer you to a mental health specialist if necessary. It's essential to find professionals who have experience with or specialize in working with autistic adults, as they are more likely to understand the unique aspects of how autism can interact with mental health issues.

For many, seeking help alleviates current distress and builds a foundation for long-term emotional resilience. By taking steps to understand and manage one's mental health, one addresses immediate concerns and invests in future well-being.

In this chapter, we have explored how to identify and respond to signs of anxiety and depression, highlighting the importance of self-monitoring and understanding when professional help is needed. Equipping yourself with these tools and knowledge enables you to navigate your mental health with greater confidence and insight, ensuring you can meet challenges with strength and resilience.

MANAGEMENT TECHNIQUES THAT WORK

Managing stress is not just about reacting when you feel overwhelmed; it's about creating an environment and lifestyle that helps you prevent the buildup of tension in the first place. Specific stress management techniques can be particularly beneficial for autistic adults, incorporating sensory-friendly practices that cater to your unique needs. Let's explore some tailored relaxation techniques, the stabilizing power of routine, cognitive-behavioral strategies specifically adapted for autistic individuals, and how to set up emergency protocols for acute stress situations.

Tailored Relaxation Techniques

Relaxation techniques that incorporate sensory integration methods can be incredibly effective. These techniques might include activities that provide deep pressure, like weighted blankets or vests, which many find soothing. Pressure can help reduce anxiety and provide a grounding effect, making you feel secure and calm. Sensory integration activities can also involve tactile items such as stress balls or soft, textured materials that you can touch, which help divert your focus from stressful stimuli and redirect it toward a calming sensory experience.

Structured relaxation exercises are another beneficial approach. These might include guided imagery, where you're led through a visualized journey to a peaceful place. Progressive muscle relaxation is when you tense and then relax different muscle groups. These exercises help reduce physical tension and aid in centering your thoughts, pulling your mind away from stressors and toward peaceful imagery or the physical sensation of relaxation. Setting aside specific times during the day for these activities can enhance their effectiveness, making relaxation a part of your daily routine.

Routine as a Stress Reducer

A predictable routine can significantly reduce stress by providing a reliable daily structure. Predictability can be soothing, reducing the anxiety that comes from uncertainty. To establish a routine, start by outlining a structure for your day, including set times for waking up, meals, work or activities, relaxation, and sleep. Within this framework, incorporate regular breaks for short relaxation exercises or sensory activities, ensuring that you have opportunities to decompress throughout the day.

It's also helpful to have set routines for particularly stressful times of the day or week. For example, if transitioning from work to home in the evenings is challenging, create a decompression routine that might include listening to calming music on the drive home and a few minutes of relaxation exercises once you arrive. Over time, these routines become signals to your body and mind, cueing them to begin the relaxation process and making the transition smoother and less stressful.

Cognitive Behavioral Techniques

Cognitive behavioral strategies can be tailored to address the specific challenges autistic adults face. One effective technique is thought challenging, which involves identifying and disputing irrational or harmful thoughts contributing to stress. For instance, if you find yourself thinking, I can never do anything right, challenge this by reflecting on past successes or aspects of the task you can handle. This helps reshape your thought patterns, making them more positive and less stress-inducing.

Behavioral experiments are another cognitive behavioral strategy where you test the accuracy of your negative predictions about a situation. For example, if you're anxious about attending a social event, you might aim to stay for a certain amount of time or speak to a specific number of people. Afterward, you can assess whether the outcomes were as adverse as anticipated. Often, you'll find that your predictions were more harmful than the reality, which can decrease your stress and anxiety about similar situations in the future.

Emergency Stress Protocols

Having a plan in place for acute stress episodes can significantly improve your ability to manage sudden spikes in anxiety or stress. Start by identifying activities or tools that have a strong calming effect on you. This could be a particular relaxation exercise, a sensory object, or a safe space where you can retreat to regain your composure.

Create a step-by-step plan that outlines exactly what to do when you feel overwhelmed. This might include moving to a quieter environment, using deep breathing techniques, or calling a designated support person—a friend, family member, or therapist who understands your stress triggers and can help talk you through the episode. Having this plan written down or saved on your phone ensures that even in moments of high stress, you won't have to think about what to do next—you can follow the steps laid out, allowing you to manage the situation more effectively.

By incorporating these stress management strategies into your life, you can handle stress more effectively and enhance your overall well-being. Each technique offers a way to reduce the impact of stressors and can be adapted to fit your unique needs and preferences, ensuring that you have the tools necessary to maintain your mental health and emotional resilience.

THERAPY AND COUNSELING: FINDING THE RIGHT HELP

Therapy can be a powerful tool for managing mental health, especially when tailored to fit the unique experiences of autistic adults. Various types of therapy, such as cognitive behavioral therapy (CBT), psychotherapy, and specialized autism therapies, offer different approaches, each with its own benefits. CBT, for instance, is structured and focuses on identifying and changing specific thought patterns and behaviors contributing to emotional distress. It's efficient if you're dealing with anxiety or depression, as it provides valuable tools to manage these conditions daily. Psychotherapy, on the other hand, often explores deeper emotional issues and can help you understand and process your feelings, which can be particularly useful if you have experienced trauma or have long-standing emotional difficulties.

Specialized therapies for autism, such as social skills therapy or sensory integration therapy, are designed to address the specific challenges that can come with being on the spectrum. These therapies can help you manage sensory overload, improve communication skills, and navigate social interactions more effectively. The key is to find a treatment that resonates with your personal needs and goals, which can significantly enhance its effectiveness in improving your mental health and overall well-being.

Seeking the right therapist who is experienced in working with autistic adults is crucial. The right therapist can make a significant difference in easing your comfort level and the success of the therapy. Start by searching for therapists who advertise their experience with autism or are part of networks specializing in autism therapy. Websites of professional organizations for psychologists or counselors usually have directories where you can search for therapists by location and type of treatment you are looking for. Once you find potential therapists, don't hesitate to ask them about their experience with autistic clients and their approach to treatment. Questions like, "How do you tailor your methods to suit autistic adults? What challenges have you encountered while working with autistic individuals, and how have you addressed them?" can provide insights into whether a therapist will be a good fit for you.

Preparing for therapy sessions can also enhance their benefit. Before starting therapy, consider what you hope to achieve and set clear, manageable goals. These could range from wanting to handle anxiety better, improving relationships, or developing better coping strategies for stress. Discuss your goals with your therapist to ensure they understand your expectations and can plan the sessions accordingly. It's also helpful to know what to expect during therapy sessions. Typical sessions might involve discussing your feelings, working through specific exercises, or exploring past experiences that might impact your current mental health.

Effective communication with your therapist is essential. If verbal communication is challenging for you, consider asking if you can use written forms of communication, like email or text, where you might feel more comfortable expressing yourself. If you're sensitive to sensory inputs, discuss this with your therapist to ensure a relaxed therapy environment. This could involve adjusting the lighting in the therapy room, having sessions when you feel most alert and calm, or even having the option to use sensory tools during sessions, like stress balls or fidget devices.

Adapting therapy sessions to suit your needs better can be a game-changer. Some autistic adults might find traditional 50-minute sessions too long, which could lead to sensory overload or fatigue. If this is the case, you might ask about the possibility of shorter or more frequent sessions. Additionally, if you have specific areas of challenge, such as sensory issues or difficulty with nonverbal communication, ensure your therapist understands these and integrates strategies to address them into your sessions.

By finding the correct type of therapy and therapist, preparing adequately, and ensuring sessions are adapted to your needs, therapy can become a valuable space for growth and healing. It's a proactive step toward managing challenges and building a more prosperous, fulfilling life where you feel more in control and supported.

SELF-CARE STRATEGIES FOR EMOTIONAL RESILIENCE

Self-care is not just a trendy concept; it's a fundamental practice, especially for autistic adults, who often encounter unique emotional and sensory challenges daily. It's about taking proactive steps to care for your mental, emotional, and physical health, fostering emotional resilience, and helping you manage and recover from stress more effectively. This approach respects your sensory needs and personal order, significantly enhancing your quality of life and giving you the tools to handle whatever comes your way with greater ease and confidence.

Consider the array of self-care activities that specifically cater to different sensory needs. If tactile sensations are significant for you, activities like clay sculpting, gardening, or even petting an animal can provide comforting touch feedback that calms and centers your mind. For those who find auditory relaxation helpful, listening to soothing sounds such as soft music, nature sounds, or white noise can provide a serene backdrop to daily activities or serve as a focused relaxation session. Visual arts, on the other hand, offer a visual and kinesthetic outlet for expression and stress relief. Engaging in painting, drawing, or photography allows you to channel emotions nonverbally, creating something beautiful and therapeutic from your feelings.

Incorporating special interests and hobbies into your self-care routine can also be incredibly beneficial. These activities are not just pastimes; they are vital for your emotional well-being, providing a source of joy, relaxation, and a sense of accomplishment. Whether assembling model trains, coding software, gardening, or studying the stars, your special interests can be a powerful self-care tool. They allow you to immerse yourself in something you love, providing a break from stress and a means of engaging deeply with something that captivates your passion. This engagement boosts your mood and reinforces your self-esteem by reminding you of your skills and creativity.

Setting limitations is another crucial aspect of self-care. It involves understanding and communicating your limits regarding how much social interaction, sensory stimulation, and various activities you can handle without feeling overwhelmed. Learning to say "no" is a powerful tool in managing your energy and preventing burnout. It's not about being uncooperative but respecting your needs and ensuring you don't overextend yourself. Whether declining an invitation that feels overwhelming, requesting a quiet space to work, or limiting your time on specific tasks, boundary setting helps protect your well-being by keeping stress levels manageable and ensuring you have the energy for your self-care practices.

Moreover, recognizing when your limits are being approached or exceeded is vital in taking proactive steps to address your needs before becoming overwhelmed. This awareness allows you to implement coping strategies effectively, such as taking a break, using sensory tools, or engaging in one of your self-care activities to restore your balance and well-being. By regularly practicing these self-care strategies, you not only enhance your ability to cope with daily stresses but also build a foundation of emotional resilience that supports a more fulfilling and balanced life.

Self-care is not a luxury but essential to maintaining your health and well-being. You create a personalized self-care routine that supports your overall happiness and resilience by choosing activities that cater to your sensory needs, incorporating your passions, and setting clear boundaries. This proactive approach to managing stress and enhancing your well-being is not just about surviving; it's about thriving in an overwhelming world. So, take time to nurture yourself; it's not just beneficial. It's necessary for a vibrant, fulfilling life.

NAVIGATING MENTAL HEALTH SERVICES AS AN AUTISTIC ADULT

Navigating the mental health care system can often feel like trying to decode a complex map with few clear directions. For autistic adults, understanding this system, including your rights and how to advocate for yourself effectively, is crucial. The mental health care system encompasses a range of services and providers, including psychologists, psychiatrists, counselors, and specialized therapists. Each plays a different role in supporting mental health, and understanding who to approach and when can greatly enhance your ability to get the support you need.

Your rights to accommodations under the law are important to navigating the mental health system. Laws such as the Americans with Disabilities Act (ADA) in the United States ensure that you have access to necessary modifications that can help you fully participate in mental health care. This might include longer appointment times, having information provided in written formats, or ensuring no physical barriers in clinics or offices. Familiarizing yourself with these rights can empower you to request adjustments that can make therapy more accessible and effective for you.

Advocating for yourself when interacting with mental health professionals is another critical skill. It involves clearly articulating your needs and ensuring they are understood and respected. This might mean explaining your autism in ways that might not be immediately apparent to someone unfamiliar, such as needing more time to process information or communicate your thoughts. It's also about asking for specific accommodations to participate fully in therapy, such as having sessions simultaneously each week to maintain a predictable routine or requesting breaks during sessions if you experience sensory overload.

Building a support network can significantly impact your mental health journey. This network can include peers who share similar experiences, family members who support your needs, or specialized support groups that provide a space to connect with others who understand your challenges. These networks can offer practical advice, emotional support, and an incredibly comforting sense of community. They can also be valuable for sharing information about the mental health system and finding supportive therapists or services.

Accessing community and online resources designed for autistic adults can also provide support. Many organizations offer hotlines, websites, and local services that can help you understand your options for therapy and support. These resources often provide information about local mental health professionals experienced in working with autistic adults, as well as tips for preparing for treatment and what to expect from mental health services. Engaging with these resources can help you find the right help and build a broader understanding of managing your mental health effectively.

Navigating the mental health system as an autistic adult involves understanding the landscape of services available, knowing your rights, advocating for your needs, building a supportive network, and utilizing community resources. By developing skills in these areas, you can enhance your ability to access and benefit from mental health services, supporting your overall well-being and ability to thrive.

As we wrap up this exploration of mental health services, remember that understanding and navigating this complex system is a powerful step toward taking control of your mental health. The knowledge and strategies discussed here can equip you with the tools needed to advocate for yourself and ensure you receive the support you deserve. The journey continues to empower you to live a fulfilling and balanced life, enriched by a deeper understanding of managing and advocating for your mental health needs.

CHAPTER 7
ADVOCACY AND EMPOWERMENT

Navigating the intricacies of advocacy and empowerment as an autistic adult can sometimes feel like assembling a complex puzzle without a reference picture. It's about understanding where each piece fits—legal rights, educational accommodations, or social entitlements—and how you can use these pieces to build a life that accommodates and celebrates your unique way of experiencing the world. This chapter aims to guide you through understanding your rights and how to assert them, empowering you to advocate for yourself in various aspects of life.

UNDERSTANDING YOUR RIGHTS AS AN AUTISTIC ADULT

Legal Protections and Rights

Living with autism should never mean less access to opportunities or rights than anyone else. In the United States, the Americans with Disabilities Act (ADA) and the Disability

Discrimination Act (DDA) serve as robust legal shields, protecting individuals with disabilities—including those on the autism spectrum—from discrimination in many areas of public life. These laws ensure that people with disabilities have equal rights in employment, education, public accommodations, and more. For instance, the ADA prohibits discrimination in all employment practices, including job application procedures, hiring, firing, advancement, compensation, training, and other terms, conditions, and privileges of employment. It also requires employers to provide reasonable accommodations to qualified individuals with disabilities unless doing so would cause undue hardship.

Understanding these laws is crucial because it teaches you to navigate situations where your rights might be challenged. For example, if you're applying for a job and need accommodations for the interview process, knowing that the ADA supports your right to these accommodations can give you the confidence to request them. Similarly, the DDA provides protections that ensure you are not discriminated against in educational settings, allowing access to the support and resources needed to achieve your academic goals.

Educational Rights and Accommodations

Education is a fundamental right, and being on the autism spectrum should not deter you from accessing quality education and the opportunities that come with it. Under laws like the ADA, educational institutions are required to provide reasonable accommodation to students with disabilities. This accommodation might include extended time for test-taking, a quiet exam room, note-taking services, or the ability to use technology aids in the classroom.

If you are in an educational setting and struggling without accommodations or are unsure what accommodations might help, contact your institution's disability services. These offices can help you navigate the process of documenting your disability and determining which accommodations will support your specific needs. Engaging with these services helps tailor your educational experience to your needs and ensures you have the support necessary to succeed academically.

Rights in Public and Social Settings

Your rights extend beyond education and employment into all public and social realms. The ADA ensures you can access public spaces and participate in community activities like anyone else. This includes the right to access public transportation, government services, parks, and theaters, all of which should be accessible and inclusive.

Moreover, reasonable accommodations in these settings are not just about physical access but also include considerations for sensory sensitivities or communication preferences. For instance, if attending a public event, you might request advance notice of loud noises or areas where you can take a break if the environment becomes overwhelming.

Advocating for Your Rights

One of the most powerful skills you can develop is advocating for yourself. It starts with understanding your rights and then effectively communicating your needs. When you find yourself in a situation where you need to advocate for your rights, start by clearly stating your needs and the reasons for them. Be direct, and, if possible, suggest practical solutions. For example, if you need specific accommodation at work, explain how this accommodation will help you perform your job effectively.

Sometimes, despite your best efforts, you might encounter resistance or a lack of understanding. In these cases, knowing how to escalate your concerns appropriately is important. This might involve filing a complaint with the relevant authorities, seeking advice from legal professionals who specialize in disability rights, or reaching out to advocacy organizations that can offer support and guidance.

Textual Element: Advocacy Checklist

- **Know your rights.** Familiarize yourself with the relevant laws like the ADA and DDA.
- **Document your needs**. Keep records of accommodations you require and why it is necessary.
- **Communicate clearly**. When requesting accommodations, be clear about what you need and why.

- **Seek support**. Engage with advocacy groups or legal counsel if you encounter discrimination.

Empowering yourself through advocacy affects your life and paves the way for greater understanding and inclusivity for others in the autism community. By standing up for your rights, you contribute to a broader effort to ensure that society recognizes and respects the diverse needs of all its members.

Effective Self-Advocacy in the Workplace

Navigating the workplace as an autistic adult involves more than just managing your job responsibilities—it also means knowing how to advocate for yourself effectively. This includes making decisions about disclosure and requesting accommodations that allow you to perform to your best ability. Deciding whether to disclose your autism diagnosis at work is a deeply personal choice and one that comes with various considerations. On the one hand, being open about your diagnosis can pave the way for obtaining necessary accommodations, such as a quiet workspace or flexible scheduling, which can significantly improve your work experience. On the other hand, there's an understandable concern about potential biases or misunderstandings from colleagues or supervisors.

If you choose to disclose, planning how to communicate this information is important. Prepare by outlining the key points you want to convey, focusing on how understanding your needs can lead to improved performance and a more harmonious workplace. For instance, you might explain that working in a quieter part of the office helps you focus better, enhancing your productivity. Be clear and specific about what you need and why when requesting accommodations. Suggesting practical solutions is helpful, showing that you've thought about the easiest ways to implement these changes without disrupting the workflow.

Assertive communication is key in these interactions. This doesn't mean being aggressive; it's about being straightforward, calm, and direct. Practice phrases like, "Having a set schedule helps me manage my day more effectively, which means I can meet my targets more reliably." Such statements articulate your needs while also highlighting the benefits to your employer. Remember, the goal of accommodations is to enable you to perform your job to the best of your ability, which ultimately benefits the company.

Building Alliances at Work

Creating supportive relationships within your workplace can significantly ease the process of self-advocacy. Allies can be coworkers, supervisors, or even human resources personnel who understand your needs and support your contributions to the team. Start by identifying colleagues who empathize and understand diversity and inclusion initiatives. You can gradually build rapport through regular interactions, sharing small personal insights, or collaborating on projects. As these relationships strengthen, you may find it easier to discuss your needs more openly, knowing that you have allies who appreciate your strengths and understand your challenges.

Moreover, these alliances can be instrumental if you encounter resistance or misunderstanding about your accommodation request. Having colleagues who can vouch for your work ethic and the positive impact of previous accommodations can be incredibly persuasive. They can also offer social support, making your workplace bearable and enjoyable. Building these relationships takes time and trust, and it's most effective when approached with sincerity and mutual respect.

Handling Discrimination and Conflicts

Despite your best efforts, you might encounter situations where you face discrimination or conflict related to your autism. It's crucial to know how to handle these challenges professionally and assertively. First, document all incidents thoroughly, noting dates, times, locations, and the individuals involved. This documentation can be vital to escalate the issue to HR or take legal action.

When facing conflict, address the issue directly with the person involved if you feel safe doing so. Calmly explain how their actions or words affect you, using specific examples. Sometimes, people are unaware of the impact of their behavior and are willing to make changes once they understand the issue.

If the situation doesn't improve or you face outright discrimination, seeking support from human resources or higher authority within your organization is appropriate. They ensure that all employees have a safe and equitable work environment. If you're a union member, they can also provide support and guidance on proceedings.

In cases where internal resolutions are ineffective, you might consider seeking external support from organizations specializing in advocacy for autistic individuals. They can offer guidance on your rights and next steps, including legal action if necessary.

Navigating advocacy in the workplace requires a balance of clear communication, strategic disclosure, and building supportive networks. By understanding and asserting your rights and fostering positive relationships at work, you can create a work environment that not only accommodates your needs but also values and leverages your unique strengths.

Navigating Healthcare Communicating with Professionals

Managing healthcare interactions effectively is crucial for receiving the best possible care and ensuring your needs are met, especially when you have specific concerns like those associated with autism. Preparing for medical appointments can significantly impact the efficiency and outcome of these visits. Start by taking time before your appointment to write down any symptoms you've been experiencing clearly, your questions, and important information about your medical history. This preparation helps ensure you don't forget to mention critical details during your appointment. It's also beneficial to list any medications you are taking, including over-the-counter drugs and supplements, as this can affect treatment options.

Bringing a friend, family member, or advocate to your appointments can be incredibly helpful. They can provide emotional support, help you articulate your concerns, and assist in remembering the doctor's advice and instructions. Choose someone you trust and who understands your communication style and needs. If you're worried about becoming overwhelmed or forgetting to ask important questions, having this support can make a significant difference in the quality of your healthcare experience.

When it comes to communicating with healthcare providers, clarity and assertiveness are key. Ensure your doctor understands your concerns and how you experience symptoms, which might differ from typical presentations. For instance, explain how specific sensory environments in medical settings might affect your communication ability or exacerbate your symptoms. Practice concisely describing your symptoms and concerns, and don't hesitate to correct misunderstandings. If you feel your concerns are not being taken seriously, it's okay to reassert them or even consider seeking a second opinion.

Understanding medical jargon can be another barrier to effective communication in healthcare settings. Medical professionals often use specialized language that can be confusing. Don't be shy about asking your healthcare provider to explain terms or procedures in plain language. To aid in this, familiarize yourself with common medical terminologies related to your condition before your appointment. Here's a brief glossary to get you started:

- **Chronic**: Long-standing, constant. Opposite of acute.
- **Efficacy**: The ability to produce a desired or intended result.
- **Idiopathic**: Relates to any disease or condition that arises spontaneously or for unknown cause.
- **Remission**: A decrease in or disappearance of signs and symptoms of disease.

Empowering yourself with knowledge is a powerful tool that can make your interactions with healthcare providers more effective and less stressful. The more you understand about your condition and treatment options, the more confident you will feel in your discussions with your provider.

Advocating for appropriate medical care is not just important; it's essential—especially when standard treatment options may not suit you. If a proposed treatment feels uncomfortable or you believe there might be a better alternative, discuss this openly with your provider. Research treatments beforehand and come to appointments prepared with information and questions about potential options. It's important to be proactive about your health care and to remember that you have a right to be involved in all decisions about your treatment.

When advocating for yourself, be clear about your treatment goals and the outcomes you hope to achieve. This clarity can help your healthcare provider recommend care that aligns with your health objectives. If you encounter resistance or feel your needs are not adequately addressed, consider bringing in notes or documentation supporting your concerns. Sometimes, written information can help clarify complex issues more effectively than spoken communication alone.

This proactive approach to healthcare, built on preparation, clear communication, and informed self-advocacy, can help you navigate medical systems more effectively and ensure your healthcare experiences are as positive and productive as possible. By taking charge of your interactions with healthcare professionals, you empower yourself to manage your health proactively, which is integral to living well with autism.

LEGAL RIGHTS AND AUTISM: WHAT YOU NEED TO KNOW

Navigating the legal landscape can often appear taxing, especially when understanding how the laws apply to autism. Knowing your legal rights and navigating legal systems effectively is crucial for advocating for yourself and ensuring you receive fair treatment in all aspects of life. Disability law, particularly as it pertains to autism, is there to protect you and ensure that your rights are upheld in various situations, from the workplace to educational settings and beyond.

Disability laws such as the Americans with Disabilities Act (ADA) in the United States provide a framework that prohibits discrimination based on disability. This extends to all areas of public life, including jobs, schools, transportation, and all public and private places that are open to the public. The purpose of these laws is to ensure that people with disabilities, including those on the autism spectrum, have the same rights and opportunities as everyone else. Understanding these laws is not just about knowing what discrimination looks like but also about understanding the protections you are afforded under the law, which can range from reasonable accommodations at work to access to assistive technologies in educational settings.

Navigating the legal system can be particularly challenging. If you find yourself in a situation where you need legal help, whether dealing with discrimination, accessing education, or ensuring your workplace accommodations are met, knowing how to find and work with legal professionals experienced in disability rights can make a significant difference. Many legal aid organizations offer services at reduced rates or even for free for those who qualify. These organizations often have lawyers who are knowledgeable about disability laws and can provide guidance specific to your situation. It's also valuable to know about advocacy groups and nonprofit organizations that offer resources and advice on navigating legal challenges related to autism.

Participating in Legal Proceedings

Legal proceedings can be overwhelming for anyone, but if you are autistic, the typical settings and processes can be particularly challenging due to sensory sensitivities or communication differences. It's important to know that you can request accommodations to participate effectively in legal settings. For example, you may request a quieter discussion room if the noise is distracting. If long sessions are challenging, you might ask for more frequent breaks to help manage stress and maintain focus. Understanding and articulating the accommodations you need is critical to self-advocacy in legal situations.

When preparing for legal proceedings, consider all the possible barriers you might face and consider accommodations that could mitigate these challenges. Communicating these needs well before court dates or meetings is advisable. Documentation from healthcare providers that outlines your diagnosis and the accommodations you require can support your requests. This proactive approach helps ensure you can participate fully in the proceedings and sets a precedent for accommodating others in the legal system with similar needs.

Staying Informed About Legal Changes

Laws and regulations can change, and these changes can affect your rights and how you need to advocate for yourself. Staying informed about these changes is crucial. Many advocacy groups and legal organizations offer updates and analyses on current disability laws and any proposed changes. Subscribing to newsletters, attending workshops, and participating in community advocacy groups are all proactive ways to stay informed.

Educating about your rights helps you advocate for yourself and prepares you to assist others in the autism community.

Sharing your knowledge and experiences can strengthen community ties and foster a more inclusive society. Remember, being informed is a key step in being empowered, and your voice is important in the ongoing dialogue about the rights and inclusion of autistic individuals in all areas of life.

As we close this chapter on understanding and navigating your legal rights as an autistic adult, remember that these laws and systems are in place to support your ability to live a whole and equitable life. Whether advocating for reasonable accommodations at work, understanding your educational rights, or participating in legal proceedings, the knowledge you gain empowers you to stand up for yourself and others. As we move forward, let's continue to build on this foundation, ensuring that every step is toward greater understanding, advocacy, and empowerment.

CHAPTER 8
FINDING AND BUILDING SUPPORT NETWORKS

Navigating many challenges can feel like navigating a vast, uncharted sea. For individuals on the autism spectrum, the complexities add unique layers that can make this navigation seem difficult. However, imagine transforming this solitary voyage into a collaborative journey, surrounded by a fleet of supportive ships, each helmed by individuals who understand and share similar experiences. This is the essence of building strong, supportive networks. This chapter delves into the digital realms where such communities thrive, offering you the tools and insights to connect with others who can turn the journey into a shared adventure.

ONLINE SUPPORT NETWORKS: CONNECTING DIGITALLY

In the vast expanse of the internet, various online platforms serve as bustling hubs for autism support groups. These digital communities range from forums and dedicated social media groups to comprehensive websites offering numerous resources and interaction opportunities. Engaging in these spaces opens a world where geographical boundaries dissolve, allowing you to connect with peers and experts who might be continents away but are just a click away.

Exploring Online Platforms

Accessing online autism support communities can be likened to exploring a new city. Each platform has its own unique layout, culture, and etiquette. Forums, for example, often function like town squares where discussions on numerous topics flourish. Here, you can dive deep into threads that discuss everything from daily challenges and triumphs to specific advice on coping mechanisms and professional growth. Social media groups provide a more dynamic interaction, with members sharing real-time updates, personal stories, and support. Websites dedicated to autism support often serve as libraries with articles, videos, and tools tailored to help you navigate autism and adulthood.

Engaging Effectively

To engage effectively in these digital communities, consider your interactions part of a larger conversation that respects its participants' diverse experiences and perspectives. Start by introducing yourself and sharing your relevant experiences, which can help establish a connection with other members. When asking for advice, be clear and specific—this makes it easier for others to provide support and helps build enriching and constructive conversations. Remember, etiquette in digital communications is paramount; always approach interactions with kindness and respect, acknowledging what others contribute to the platform and expressing gratitude for the insights shared.

Safety and Privacy

Having the digital world and its incredible opportunities for connection, navigating it with an eye toward safety and privacy is vital. Be cautious with personal information, such as your finances, address, and phone number. Think carefully about what you share publicly. Many forums and groups offer private settings where discussions are not visible to nonmembers—these can provide safer spaces for more personal or sensitive conversations. Additionally, be aware of online scams and harassment; familiarize yourself with the platforms' safety features, such as how to report inappropriate content or block users who may be problematic. Maintaining your digital well-being is as important as finding the right community.

Benefits of Online Networks

The benefits of participating in online autism support networks are manifold. For many, these networks are lifelines—accessible sources of support and understanding available anytime, regardless of where you live. They offer a spectrum of perspectives that can enrich your knowledge of autism, providing both comfort and diverse strategies for managing day-to-day challenges. Moreover, these networks can become advocacy platforms, amplifying the voices of autistic individuals and influencing broader societal understanding and policies. The strength of an online community lies in its collective wisdom and the solidarity it fosters among its members, making the journey through adulthood more informed and less isolating.

Textual Element: Online Safety Checklist

- **Personal Information**: Always think twice before sharing personal details. Limit what you share to what is necessary for the interaction.
- **Privacy Settings**: Familiarize yourself with each platform's privacy settings. Adjust settings to control who can see your posts and personal information.
- **Reporting Tools**: Learn how to use the platform's reporting tools to report harassment or inappropriate content.
- **Secure Websites**: Ensure that websites are secure (look for HTTPS:// in the URL) when accessing forums or groups, particularly when sharing sensitive information.

As you continue to explore and engage with these digital communities, remember that each interaction enhances your understanding and network and contributes to a larger tapestry of shared knowledge and support. By participating in these online spaces, you help weave a network that stretches across the globe, providing support and understanding to countless others on the autism spectrum.

LOCAL SUPPORT GROUPS: FINDING THE RIGHT FIT

Venturing into the realm of local support groups can be as enriching as it is unnerving. The idea of walking into a room with strangers, even if they share similar experiences, might stir a mix of anxiety and anticipation. However, these groups often become the cornerstone of personal support networks, offering camaraderie, insights, and a shared space for growth and understanding. To navigate this landscape effectively, knowing where to look for these groups, how to assess their suitability, and the best ways to integrate into these communities is important.

Identifying Local Resources

Finding the right local support group often starts with detective work. Begin your search by tapping into readily available but usually overlooked resources. Local libraries, for instance, frequently host or have information about community support groups and might even offer meeting spaces for such gatherings. Community centers are another invaluable resource, serving as hubs for various social groups that cater to diverse interests and needs, including support groups for those on the autism spectrum.

You might also consider contacting local health services or therapists specializing in autism. Professionals in the field are usually well-connected and might have information on existing groups or be interested in helping to start one. Additionally, universities or colleges often have psychology or counseling departments where support groups might be offered as part of outreach programs or as initiatives led by students in related fields. Don't overlook the power of the internet here; a quick search can yield information about local organizations or networks that list support groups on their websites.

Assessing the Fit

Once you've located a few potential groups, it's crucial to determine the right fit. Start by considering the size of the group. Smaller groups might offer a more intimate setting, which can be less intimidating and allow for deeper connections. On the other hand, larger groups might provide many opportunities and a wider range of experiences but could feel overwhelming if you prefer more personal interactions. Giving both settings a try will help you determine which is the best fit.

Next, examine the focus topics of the meetings. Some groups might concentrate on social skills, others might discuss employment challenges, and some might offer a more general support format. Think about what you hope to gain from the group. If you're looking for specific advice or coping strategies, a group with a targeted focus might be more beneficial. The number of meetings is also important; regular meetings can provide consistent support and help build long-term relationships.

Trial and Participation

Taking a trial approach to participation can alleviate some of the pressure. Allow yourself to attend a few sessions without any commitment to continue long term. This approach lets you get a feel for the group's dynamics, the regularity of the members, and the overall atmosphere without feeling bound to return. It's normal to feel a bit out of place at first. Remember, everyone in the room likely had a first day filled with their apprehensions.

During these initial visits, observe how the meetings are conducted and how members interact with each other. Are the discussions open and respectful? Is there a facilitator or leader who ensures that everyone gets a chance to speak? These factors contribute significantly to the group's overall effectiveness and comfort level. Don't be discouraged if you decide the group is not what you want. It's perfectly okay to try out several groups before finding the right one.

Building Local Connections

The relationships you build within a support group can extend beyond the scheduled meetings, leading to friendships and a supportive community network that's invaluable in times of need or crisis. Engage actively with the group; share your experiences and listen to others. Often, these interactions can lead to mutual support that is both empowering and comforting.

Creating these connections can also provide practical benefits, such as learning about local resources or opportunities for advocacy that you might not have discovered on your own. As you become more involved, you might find ways to contribute to the group by sharing your insights, helping organize meetings, or offering support to newer members. This active participation enriches your experience and enhances the group's cohesion and resourcefulness.

As you explore and engage with local support groups, remember that the goal is to find a community where you feel understood and valued. Each group you try is a step toward understanding what works best for you, and each interaction is an opportunity for both sides to learn, grow, and appreciate the unique journey of living with autism.

BUILDING A SUPPORT NETWORK FROM SCRATCH

Sometimes, the existing support groups in your area might not quite match your needs or those of your community. Perhaps they're too general, too far away, or they meet at times that are inconvenient for you. When faced with such a scenario, one empowering option is to start your own support group. This initiative provides the tailored support you seek and gives back to others in your community who might be experiencing similar challenges.

Starting a Support Confidently

The first step in creating a support group is to define its purpose and scope. What specific needs will it address? Will it focus on adults with autism generally, or perhaps on topics such as employment, relationships, or navigating daily challenges? Once the focus is clear, is securing a venue next? Your local community centers, libraries, or even places of worship often have spaces available for community groups and may offer them for free or a nominal fee. Ensure that the space is accessible and comfortable, considering sensory sensitivities that might be common among group members.

Setting a schedule that works for potential members is crucial. Planning based on personal availability might be tempting, but it's more effective to survey the community to find times that work for a majority. This could be done through simple online tools like Doodle polls or Google Forms. Promoting your group is the next step, and it can be approached creatively. Flyers in community centers, posts on local online forums, and word of mouth through therapists or local clinicians are all viable strategies. Social media can also be a powerful tool for reaching a wider audience.

Managing group dynamics plays a critical role in the group's long-term success. Establishing ground rules in the initial meetings ensures that discussions remain respectful and productive. Consider what roles might be needed to keep the group organized and engaging. For instance, besides being a facilitator, you might want roles for handling logistics, communication, or welcoming new members.

Leveraging Community Resources

Community resources can provide substantial support for a new group. Engage local businesses that might be willing to support the group through funding, resources, or even promotional help. For instance, a local café might host meetups, or a printing business might offer to print flyers at a discount. Community boards, both online and in physical locations, are excellent for advertising meetings and events.

Local universities or colleges can be particularly valuable resources. Students in relevant fields such as psychology, social work, or education might be interested in participating in or helping manage the group as part of their studies. This can add a valuable dimension to the group, bringing fresh ideas and the latest academic perspectives.

Setting Goals and Objectives

Clear goals and objectives guide the group's activities and help measure its success and areas for improvement. Start by establishing what the group aims to achieve in the short and long term. The aim is to provide emotional support, educate its members about coping strategies, or perhaps advocate for local changes. Setting these goals early on and revisiting them regularly ensures that the group remains focused and effective. It also helps keep the group aligned with the members' needs, adapting as they evolve.

Sustaining the Group

Keeping a support group active and engaging over time requires ongoing effort. One key element is fostering strong leadership. While it might start with one or two people, developing leadership skills within the group ensures that it doesn't rely on just one person and can continue to thrive even as members come and go. Regularly scheduled meetings, consistent communication, and shared responsibilities help maintain the group's momentum.

Member turnover is natural, so creating a welcoming environment for new members is essential for sustainability. Having a buddy system or mentorship arrangements can help integrate new members. Regularly asking for feedback and ideas for activities can keep existing members engaged and ensure the group continues to meet their needs.

By taking the initiative to start and sustain a support group, you not only create a valuable resource for yourself and others but also contribute to a stronger, more interconnected community. This proactive approach not only meets the immediate needs of its members but also builds a foundation of support and understanding that can enrich the lives of all involved.

LEVERAGING SOCIAL MEDIA FOR COMMUNITY ENGAGEMENT

Social media has many great things to offer. It'sn't just a tool for staying updated or sharing snippets of daily life; it's a powerful platform for creating and nurturing support networks, especially for the autism community. By understanding how to use social media strategically, you can transform your feeds into vibrant support, advocacy, and connection forums. Whether you're aiming to build a local group or connect with global voices, the approach to engaging on these platforms can significantly influence your success.

Using Social Media Strategically

The strategic use of social media begins with identifying the right platforms that resonate with your target audience. For instance, if you focus on sharing detailed stories or articles, platforms like Facebook or blogs can be more suitable because their format supports longer content. Conversely, Instagram and Twitter might be your go-to platforms for sharing visuals or short, impactful messages. Once you've selected the right platforms, content creation is next. Content that resonates with your audience usually balances between being informative and relatable. Share stories that talk about challenges and celebrate victories—big and small.

Engagement is key in social media. It's not just about posting content but also interacting with followers. Respond to comments, participate in discussions, and engage with other users' content. This two-way interaction helps build a community that feels valued and heard. Additionally, consider organizing live sessions or Q&A segments, which can provide a direct way to engage and address the community's concerns or questions. This real-time interaction adds a personal touch and can strengthen the community bond.

Creating Inclusive Online Spaces

Creating an inclusive online space requires thoughtful moderation and clear communication of group rules. Establish guidelines that promote respect and constructive dialogue. It's essential that all members feel safe to express themselves without fear of judgment or negativity. Moderation plays a critical role here; ensure clear procedures for addressing conflicts or inappropriate behavior. This might include having dedicated moderators trained to handle online interactions sensitively and effectively.

In managing these spaces, transparency is crucial. Regularly communicate with your community about the rules and the reasons behind them. This openness fosters trust and encourages members to take personal responsibility for maintaining the community's character. Handling conflicts or sensitive topics requires a balanced approach—addressing issues promptly and fairly, ensuring that all sides are heard, and finding resolutions reinforcing your community's values.

Digital Advocacy

Digital advocacy involves using social media platforms to raise awareness and advocate for changes that can improve the lives of those within the autism community. This can range from small-scale actions like awareness campaigns about sensory overload to more significant advocacy movements pushing for policy changes. Clarity and a call to action are essential when crafting your advocacy messages. Clearly state the issue, why it matters, and how others can help or get involved. Use compelling visuals and narratives to underscore your message, making it informative and vibrant.

Utilize hashtags to increase the visibility of your campaigns. Well-chosen hashtags can help rally the community and spread the message beyond your immediate followers. Engage with influencers or prominent community figures who can help amplify your message. Their endorsement can lend credibility and a broader reach to your advocacy efforts.

Networking Across Platforms

Consider networking across multiple social media platforms to maximize your reach and impact. Each platform has unique strengths and audience demographics, and by cross-promoting content across these platforms, you can engage a broader audience. For instance, you might use Instagram to share compelling visuals or stories and direct followers to Facebook for more detailed discussions or articles. Integrating social media with offline activities can provide a cohesive community experience. Promote local meetups, workshops, or conferences on your social platforms and vice versa, and use offline events to encourage participation in your online activities.

Leveraging social media for community engagement involves a strategic blend of content creation, inclusive space management, digital advocacy, and networking. By honing these strategies, you can transform your social media presence into a dynamic tool that fosters support, drives change, and builds a resilient community that spans the globe. As you continue to engage and grow your digital networks, remember that each post and interaction is a building block in the larger structure of support and advocacy you are creating.

SUPPORT FOR FAMILIES AND PARTNERS

Navigating life with autism involves the individual and their entire support network, including families and partners who play pivotal roles. Understanding how to share this journey effectively can enhance relationships and foster a supportive environment that benefits everyone involved. Family members and partners must understand the nuances of autism to provide support that respects the individual's needs and promotes their well-being. Every day is a learning experience for everyone.

Educating Family and Partners

Educating those closest to you about autism is foundational in building a supportive family dynamic. It's about more than recounting symptoms; it involves sharing insights into how sensory issues might affect behavior or explaining why specific social interactions can be challenging. Resources such as books, articles, and videos that accurately depict autism can be beneficial. Workshops and seminars can also offer family members and partners firsthand knowledge and strategies from experts in the field. When everyone understands the "whys" behind certain behaviors or needs, it fosters empathy and tailor-made support that can make all the difference.

Creating educational moments can also occur in everyday interactions. For instance, after a sensory overload incident, discussing what happened and exploring better coping strategies can be an enlightening experience for all involved. This educates and affects families and partners in managing and understanding autism, making them active and informed supporters rather than bystanders.

Creating Family Support Systems

Constructing robust support systems within the family structure is about creating an environment where the autistic family member feels understood and supported. This can be achieved by establishing family meetings where everyone discusses their needs and how they can help each other. During these meetings, discuss and plan routine activities and address any changes that might need to be made better to suit the family and the member with autism.

Creating communication plans is also vital. The immediate family's input can be very beneficial in figuring out ways to solve and avoid potential problems. These plans can outline how to best communicate with each other, considering the autistic family member's communication preferences and needs. For example, some might find direct communication overwhelming and prefer written methods like texts or emails, allowing them to process information at their own pace.

Establishing routines is particularly beneficial as they can provide predictability and structure, which can be comforting for someone with autism. These routines might include specific daily schedules, rules for household chores, or even rituals for family activities, which can help reduce anxiety and ensure that the household runs smoothly.

Engaging Families in Support Groups

Encouraging the involvement of families and partners in autism support groups can significantly enhance their understanding and empathy. Participating in these groups allows them to hear other perspectives, learn new strategies, and share their experiences, which can be incredibly validating. Many support groups offer sessions or events specifically designed for families and partners, which can be an excellent opportunity for them to connect with others in similar situations—possibly helping to reduce stress, resentment, and anger over the situation.

These experiences can also help alleviate feelings of isolation that family members or partners might feel. Understanding that they are not alone in their experiences can be a powerful realization, providing comfort and a support network. Additionally, these interactions can broaden their understanding of autism, providing them with a broader range of strategies and insights that can be applied in their relationships.

Support for Non-Autistic Family Members

While much focus is understandably placed on supporting the autistic individual, the well-being of non-autistic family members is also crucial. They often face their own set of challenges and emotions as they navigate life with an autistic loved one. Providing them with their support mechanisms is essential. This can include access to respite care, which allows them time to rest and recharge, or counseling services that can help them process their feelings and challenges. Communication from day one is vital in keeping the family together and dealing with emotions as they develop. Their life has been dramatically impacted compared to their friends, and acknowledgment is essential in maintaining harmony in the family unit.

Information and resources specifically tailored for non-autistic family members can also be invaluable. These resources can offer insights into how best to support their autistic loved one while also taking care of their own mental and emotional health. Support groups for family members can be a lifeline, offering a space to share experiences and strategies, reducing feelings of isolation, and enhancing their capacity to provide support.

As we conclude this exploration into family and partner involvement in the autism journey, it's clear that education, communication, and mutual support are the cornerstones of a solid and supportive network. By fostering an environment where understanding and empathy flourish, families can not only navigate the challenges of autism more effectively but also celebrate the unique perspectives and experiences it brings.

This chapter has provided insights and strategies to enhance the support systems surrounding individuals with tools, preparing them for broader challenges and opportunities. As we move into the next chapter, we will explore how personal interests and hobbies can be leveraged for personal development and community engagement, further enriching the lives of those on the autism spectrum and their networks.

CHAPTER 9
SPECIAL INTERESTS AND PERSONAL DEVELOPMENT

Imagine finding something that captures your attention and fuels your spirit, offering solace and a sense of purpose. For many, this comes in the form of special interests or passions that resonate deeply, making every day more colorful and meaningful. This chapter will explore identifying, cultivating, and integrating these special interests into your life, enhancing your personal and social identity, and maintaining enthusiasm over time.

IDENTIFYING AND CULTIVATING SPECIAL INTERESTS

Discovering and nurturing your passions isn't just about filling your time; it's about enriching your life. Whether these interests lie in art, science, music, technology, or any other field, they hold the potential to transform mundane activities into moments of joy and fulfillment. Identifying these interests often starts with a spark—a moment of curiosity or excitement that feels different from everyday interests.

Introspection plays a key role in unearthing these passions. Consider journaling as a tool to delve into your thoughts and feelings. Regularly writing down what activities you find absorbing or what topics you keep returning to can provide clear patterns that might indicate a particular interest. Experimenting with new activities can also open doors to unexpected passions. It could be as simple as joining a local workshop, trying out a new hobby, or attending a lecture on a topic outside of your usual interests. The key is to remain open and curious, allowing yourself to experience and explore without preconceptions.

Once you pinpoint a potential interest, the next step is to nurture it. Setting small, achievable goals is a practical approach to gradually deepening your engagement without feeling overwhelmed. For example, suppose you discover a keen interest in astronomy. In that case, your initial goals might include reading one new article about space each week or observing the night sky using a basic telescope. As your interest grows, these goals can evolve into more complex projects, such as joining an amateur astronomy club or contributing to a community stargazing event.

Connecting with others who share your interests can significantly enhance your experience and provide a network of support and inspiration. This might involve joining online forums and local clubs or attending meetups and conventions. Engaging with experts in the field can also provide deeper insights and learning opportunities that books or online resources cannot offer. These connections not only facilitate learning but also help in building a community that shares your passion.

Encouraging Persistent Engagement

Maintaining enthusiasm for any interest requires effort, especially when faced with challenges such as limited resources or waning motivation. One effective way to sustain engagement is to integrate your interests into your daily routine. For instance, if you're passionate about writing, you could set a daily time to write, even if it's just a few sentences. This consistency turns occasional interest into a lasting part of your life.

Overcoming resource limitations can also be a hurdle. If affordability of materials or access to facilities is an issue, look for community resources to offer support. Many libraries provide access to tools and materials, and local community centers often offer classes at a reduced cost. For more specialized interests, online platforms can be invaluable. Websites like Coursera or Khan Academy offer free or low-cost courses on a wide range of subjects that can help you advance your knowledge and skills from the comfort of your home.

Setting long-term goals and celebrating milestones can also significantly benefit persistent engagement. Whether mastering a particular skill, completing a project, or sharing your work with others, having specific milestones to aim for can provide motivation and a sense of accomplishment. Celebrating these achievements, no matter how small, can reinforce your commitment to your interests and give you the encouragement needed to continue.

As you explore and develop your special interests, remember that these pursuits are more than hobbies. They are vital to your identity and how you connect with the world. They offer a unique outlet for expression and interaction that can enhance your sense of self and interactions with others. By embracing and integrating these interests into your life, you enrich your experience of the world, making every day a little more engaging and fulfilling.

USING SPECIAL INTERESTS TO BOOST CAREER OPPORTUNITIES

When you consider your career path, integrating your interests can transform what might be just a job into a fulfilling career. This alignment enhances job satisfaction and provides a clear edge in today's competitive job market. Let's explore how you can weave your passions into your professional life, ensuring that work feels less like a mandatory chore and more like a continuation of your interests.

Aligning your special interests with your professional goals starts with understanding how these interests can translate into job skills or even direct career paths. For instance, if you're sincerely interested in vintage comics, you might explore roles in publishing, graphic design, or work in museums and archives specializing in pop culture. Similarly, a passion for coding and technology could lead to opportunities in software development, cybersecurity, or tech support. The key lies in identifying industries and roles that value your knowledge and enthusiasm.

Think about the broader applications of your interests. Someone fascinated by drones, for example, can look beyond just piloting them for hobbies; they might consider roles in aerial photography, geographic data collection, or even in logistics companies exploring drone delivery systems. The first step is mapping out industries and companies where your interests could be a valuable asset. Then, tailor your job search and application materials to highlight how your unique interests make you an ideal candidate, aligning your passion with the needs of potential employers.

Building Skills Through Interests

Your special interests are not just hobbies; they are a powerhouse for developing professional skills employers covet. Engaging deeply with a topic you love naturally develops skills such as analytical thinking, problem-solving, creativity, and technical abilities. For example, suppose you're enthusiastic about building model airplanes. In that case, you're likely honing precision, attention to detail, and spatial reasoning skills—all valuable in fields like engineering, architecture, and design.

Consider also the soft skills that cultivating a special interest can develop. For instance, organizing a local gaming group enhances leadership, event planning, and interpersonal communication skills. Such experiences are good when you can articulate them correctly in resumes or interviews, showing potential employers that your hobbies build transferable skills beneficial in a professional setting.

To capitalize on this, take stock of the skills you've gained from your interests and consider how they apply to the jobs you're targeting. You might even find gaps that can be filled by taking your interest further, such as enrolling in advanced courses or undertaking specific projects. For instance, if you're into photography, taking a course on photo editing can refine your hobby and equip you with the skills needed for roles in marketing or digital content creation.

Networking Within Interest Areas

Networking within your interest can open doors to opportunities that might otherwise remain out of reach. Start by joining clubs, online communities, or professional associations that align with your interests. These platforms can be invaluable for connecting with like-minded individuals, sharing knowledge, and staying updated on industry trends and job openings.

Attending workshops, seminars, and conferences is also a strategic way to network. These events often bring together enthusiasts and professionals who share your passion. Make a point to engage actively during these gatherings. Asking insightful questions during sessions or sharing your experiences can make you memorable, paving the way for future professional connections.

Don't overlook the power of online platforms like LinkedIn to connect with industry leaders and peers. Participate in discussions, share articles about your interests, and contribute your posts. This visibility can attract the attention of potential employers or collaborators who value your expertise and enthusiasm.

Creating a Personal Brand

Creating a personal brand around your interests in today's digital world can significantly boost your professional visibility and opportunities. Start by defining what sets you apart and how your interests align with your professional aspirations. This unique blend becomes your brand—a reflection of your expertise and passions.

Develop a consistent message across all your professional and personal platforms. Whether it's a blog, LinkedIn profile, or even your portfolio, ensure that your passion and expertise in your interest area shine through. For instance, if you are passionate about environmental conservation, share your thoughts on sustainability practices, promote your volunteer work, and highlight any related projects you've undertaken.

Remember, every blog post you write, every project you share, and every interaction you have adds a layer to your brand. Over time, this brand builds a narrative that can make you a desirable candidate or collaborator to organizations within your field of interest. It's about making your passion visible and relatable, making what you love integral to your professional identity.

SPECIAL INTERESTS AS A COPING TOOL

Engaging deeply with your special interests isn't just a fulfilling way to spend your time—it can also be a powerful mechanism for managing stress and enhancing your emotional well-being. When you immerse yourself in activities that captivate your attention, you're not just occupying your mind but also nurturing your spirit. This engagement provides a unique form of emotional regulation, offering control over your environment and a profound sense of accomplishment. Whether painting, coding, gardening, or studying the stars, these activities can help anchor you during turbulent times, providing a reliable escape that calms your mind and soothes your soul.

The beauty of turning to your special interests during stressful times lies in their familiarity and the joy they bring. They act as safe harbors in the stormy seas of day-to-day stressors. For instance, spending an hour with your model trains or sketchbook can reset your emotional state if you feel overwhelmed by social interactions or work pressures. It's not about evading reality but giving yourself a break, a much-needed respite that allows you to return to your challenges with renewed energy and a clearer mind. This practice of turning to your passions for emotional equilibrium is something you can refine over time, integrating it more seamlessly into your daily routine. It becomes a proactive strategy for maintaining your mental health, not just a reactive measure in moments of distress.

Moreover, engaging with your interests requires focus and concentration, which can be a natural diversion from worrying thoughts or external pressures. This isn't about ignoring problems but giving your mind a break from them. Consider how a challenging puzzle or a complex craft project can absorb all your attention; in these moments, your mind gets a chance to rest from the usual anxieties and stressors that occupy it. Over time, this practice can help you develop a more resilient mindset, where you're better equipped to handle stress because you know you have a reliable outlet to regain your balance and perspective.

The therapeutic benefits of engaging in special interests are well-supported by mental health professionals. Activities that align closely with your interests can significantly boost your mood and reduce feelings of anxiety. They provide something psychologists call "flow"—a deep immersion that enhances your well-being. Regularly experiencing flow through your special interests can improve your mental health, increasing your overall life satisfaction. The key is to recognize these activities not just as hobbies but as vital components of your emotional toolkit, valuable for their ability to bring joy, reduce stress, and reinforce your sense of self.

Navigating the ups and downs of life with autism involves cultivating a suite of strategies that support your mental and emotional health. Special interests, with their dual role as sources of joy and emotional regulation tools, are a critical part of this toolkit. They allow you to take control of your emotional landscape, providing immediate relief and long-term benefits to your mental health. By recognizing and utilizing your special interests in this way, you empower yourself to lead a more balanced, fulfilling life.

BALANCING SPECIAL INTERESTS WITH DAILY RESPONSIBILITIES

Navigating the waters between diving deep into your special interests and handling the day-to-day tasks that life demands can sometimes feel like walking a tightrope. It's about finding that sweet spot where your passions enhance your life without overshadowing the essential duties that keep your world running smoothly. Whether it's managing time, setting boundaries, integrating interests into your daily routine, or maintaining a healthy perspective on your hobbies, achieving this balance is key to ensuring that your engagement in special interests remains a fulfilling part of your life rather than a source of stress.

Managing time effectively is paramount when juggling multiple responsibilities alongside your interests. Think of your time as a garden that needs careful tending—without proper management, the weeds can take over, leaving little space for the flowers to bloom. To cultivate a well-balanced schedule, assess how you currently spend your time. Keep a diary for a week, noting down all your activities. This snapshot will help you identify time leaks—those periods spent perhaps scrolling through social media or indulging in activities that don't necessarily contribute to your overall productivity or happiness. Once identified, you can reallocate some of this time toward your interests.

Another effective strategy involves using tools designed to enhance time management. Digital calendars or apps like Google Calendar or Trello can help you visually organize your tasks and set reminders for personal projects and daily responsibilities. Try blocking out specific times dedicated to your interests each day or week. This ensures regular engagement and prevents your hobbies from bleeding into time reserved for work or family. It's about creating a rhythm that accommodates your daily life's needs and the pursuits of your passions.

Setting boundaries around your particular interest activities is just as crucial as managing your time. Without clear boundaries, it's easy for these activities to encroach on other essential areas of your life, such as sleep, work, or time with loved ones. Start by defining what reasonable engagement looks like for you. For instance, you might decide that spending more than two hours daily on your hobby is too much on workdays. Communicate these boundaries to the people around you as well; letting your family or friends know about your plans can help them support you in maintaining these boundaries. Having a physical or digital "shutdown" signal is also helpful, like setting an alarm or having a specific routine that marks the end of your hobby time. This helps mentally and physically determine when to switch gears from your interests to other obligations.

Integrating your interests into your daily life rather than segmenting them into isolated chunks can also enhance how you experience your day. This integration can make daily tasks more enjoyable and ensure you engage with your passions regularly, boosting overall life satisfaction. For example, consider taking photos during your daily commute or lunch breaks if you love photography. If you're a writer, carry a notebook to jot down ideas or observations throughout the day. These small actions allow you to weave your interests into the fabric of your everyday life, enriching your daily experiences and keeping your passion alive.

Lastly, it's important to maintain a balanced perspective on your interests. While it's wonderful to have passions that excite and motivate you, keeping an obsessive focus can lead to burnout and may detract from other important areas of life. Recognize when your hobby is starting to feel like an obligation or is causing stress rather than relieving it. This awareness is crucial in taking a step back when needed. It's okay to take breaks and return with renewed energy and interest. Remember, your hobbies are a part of your life's joy —not the entirety of it. Keeping this perspective helps you enjoy your special interests sustainably, enhancing your life without overwhelming it.

By employing effective time management, setting clear boundaries, integrating interests into daily routines, and maintaining a healthy perspective, you can enjoy a rich and varied life where your responsibilities are met and your passions are fully embraced. This balance isn't just about making time for everything; it's about enriching the overall quality of your life, ensuring that each day is lived with purpose and pleasure.

COMMUNITY ENGAGING THROUGH INTERESTS

The tapestry of community life gets its color from individuals sharing their passions and strengths, creating a vibrant mosaic of interaction and mutual support. Engaging in community groups or volunteering opportunities that align with your special interests can be a profound way to connect with others, enhance your social network, and contribute meaningfully to the collective well-being. This synergy benefits the community and enriches your personal and social development.

Finding the right community group or volunteer opportunity begins with clearly understanding your interests and how they might intersect with community needs. Local community centers, nonprofit organizations, and online platforms offer a plethora of opportunities, ranging from environmental conservation groups to tech development workshops. Start by searching for groups in your area that align with your interests. Websites like Meetup.com or local Facebook groups can be excellent resources for finding community activities that resonate with your passions. Additionally, consider contacting organizations that interest you and inquire about volunteer opportunities. Often, these groups need passionate individuals with specialized knowledge or enthusiasm for their cause.

Once you find a group or project that interests you, the next step is to dive in and engage. Participating in these groups can significantly enhance your social skills, providing a platform to practice communication, teamwork, and leadership in a supportive environment. It's a space where you can share your knowledge and learn from others, creating a dynamic exchange of ideas and experiences. This engagement is particularly beneficial if social interactions are challenging; community groups offer structured social settings where interactions are guided by shared goals and activities, making communication more manageable and focused.

The benefits of community engagement extend beyond personal growth. They ripple out to influence your professional life and emotional well-being. Being actively involved in community projects can enhance your résumé, demonstrating to potential employers that you are committed, collaborative, and capable of taking initiative. Moreover, the emotional satisfaction of contributing to a cause can be immense. It provides a sense of purpose and accomplishment that is deeply fulfilling, often boosting self-esteem and counterbalance to daily life's stresses.

Contributing to the community through your special interests allows you to give back in the most impactful way—by doing what you love. Whether teaching programming skills to youth, organizing community clean-ups, or leading a local art workshop, using your passions to help others enriches your community and deepens your engagement with your interests. It's a reciprocal relationship where everyone benefits—your community gains from your skills and enthusiasm, and you enjoy seeing your passions make a tangible difference.

Volunteering also offers unique opportunities for leadership and personal growth. Many organizations allow volunteers to lead projects or teams, which can be an excellent way to develop leadership skills in a real-world context. These experiences challenge you to step out of your comfort zone, manage responsibilities, and interact with diverse groups of people, all of which are invaluable personal and professional skills. Moreover, the sense of community and belonging that comes from working with a team toward a common goal is profoundly rewarding. It reinforces your social connections and embeds you more deeply into the fabric of your community.

Engaging in community and volunteer work through your special interests presents a beautiful synergy of personal passion and public service. It allows you to explore and expand your interests in a setting that encourages learning and growth, all while contributing to the greater good. Through these activities, you develop as an individual and help cultivate a community that values cooperation, learning, and mutual support. As you continue to explore these opportunities, remember that each effort you make enhances your life and weaves a more robust, vibrant community fabric.

As this chapter closes, we reflect on the profound impact of engaging with community and volunteer work on your life and the broader social fabric. Your passions can transform your experiences and those of those around you, creating a legacy of involvement and improvement that transcends the individual. Looking ahead, we will explore how technology can further enhance and expand the reach of your interests, opening new avenues for growth and connection in an increasingly digital world.

CHAPTER 10
MAKING THE MOST OF TECHNOLOGY

In our increasingly digital world, technology serves not just as a tool for connection and creation but as a pivotal ally in orchestrating the day-to-day complexities of life, especially for individuals on the autism spectrum. For you, navigating through daily schedules, managing tasks, or keeping up with essential reminders might sometimes feel like trying to solve a puzzle without seeing the whole picture. With its precision and adaptability, this is where technology steps in like a trusted friend ready to lend a hand. Let's explore how specific apps and digital tools can transform the chaos of daily demands into a harmonized melody of order and routine.

Apps for Daily Organization and Task Management

Overview of Organizational Apps

Imagine having a personal assistant who never forgets a birthday, always knows where you've stored your notes, and can remind you of your grocery list when you enter the store. This assistant exists in organizational apps designed to simplify your life. From calendar apps that keep your appointments in check to task managers that help break down your projects into manageable steps and reminder systems that prompt you about the important little things throughout your day—these tools are indispensable for anyone looking to streamline their daily routine.

Apps like Google Calendar offer visual and auditory reminders that can be particularly useful if you forget appointments or lose track of time. Task management apps such as Asana or Trello allow you to visualize tasks as cards or lists, which you can customize and manage according to your workflow. These apps often include features like color-coding tasks, setting priority levels, or attaching files, making it easier to see what needs your attention at a glance. For those who thrive on routine, apps like Habitica gamify daily habits and tasks, turning your day-to-day responsibilities into a fun, engaging game that rewards you for completion.

Customizing Apps to Fit Individual Needs

One of the greatest strengths of technology is its flexibility. Many organizational apps offer extensive customization options for your unique needs and preferences. For instance, if you are sensitive to certain sounds or visual stimuli, many apps allow you to change notification sounds, select themes with soothing colors, or adjust the interface to reduce visual clutter. Integrating these apps with other devices, such as syncing your smartphone's task manager with your tablet or computer, ensures that you stay on top of your tasks, no matter which device you use.

Customizing your apps can involve setting specific notifications for different tasks—choosing vibrational alerts for urgent tasks or quiet, visual prompts for less critical reminders. Additionally, many apps allow you to share and collaborate on tasks with others, which can be especially helpful if you are working in a team or need family members to know your schedule or to-dos.

Benefits of Routine Building Apps

The predictability of routine can be comforting, particularly if you experience anxiety or stress about the unexpected. Apps that help build and maintain daily routines can play a crucial role in reducing such anxieties, providing a structured framework that guides you through your day. For example, routine management apps like Todoist or Microsoft To-Do can help you establish a sequence of activities that gradually become habitual, reducing the cognitive load required to plan your day from scratch each morning.

These apps help organize your time and create a balanced approach to life where time for work, relaxation, and personal interests is preplanned and safeguarded. Over time, the consistency of a well-maintained routine can improve overall time management skills, making it easier for you to find time for yourself and the things you love, reducing feelings of being overwhelmed or stressed.

Case Studies

Consider the experience of Brian, a graphic designer with autism, who found that using a task management app helped streamline his workflow and reduce work-related anxiety. By breaking down his projects into sequential tasks within the app, Brian could tackle one small task at a time, making large projects much more manageable and less taxing. Similarly, a college student, Emma, uses a routine-building app to schedule study times around her classes. The app reminds her when to switch activities, helping her maintain a healthy balance between study, leisure, and rest.

These real-life examples underscore how incorporating organizational apps into daily life can significantly enhance the ability to manage time and tasks effectively. Whether it's through creating a visual overview of your day, setting reminders for important tasks, or building a routine that supports your lifestyle, these digital tools offer practical solutions that cater to the diverse needs of individuals on the autism spectrum, making everyday life not just manageable but also more enjoyable.

TECHNOLOGY FOR NONVERBAL COMMUNICATION

In an age where technology bridges gaps and creates opportunities, it's particularly transformative for those who find verbal communication challenging. Nonverbal communication technologies, including speech-generating devices and mobile apps that translate text or symbols into speech, have opened new horizons for expressing thoughts and engaging with the world. Such innovations provide tools for communication and pathways to greater independence and community participation.

Speech-generating devices (SGDs) are among the most impactful technologies in this arena. These devices range from simple button-based systems that emit prerecorded phrases to sophisticated touch-screen gadgets that allow users to construct sentences from symbols and text. The beauty of SGDs lies in their adaptability; they can be tailored to meet individual needs. For instance, someone with a deep love for literature might personalize their device to include quotes from their favorite books, enabling them to share this passion with others. Similarly, these devices can be programmed with vocabulary specific to different environments, such as school, work, or social gatherings, making it easier for users to interact appropriately and effectively in various settings.

Mobile apps designed for nonverbal communication also play a crucial role. Apps like Proloquo2Go and TouchChat offer customizable communication boards filled with symbols and text that can be tapped to speak phrases aloud. These apps often feature robust customization options, allowing users to add photos and customize the layout to suit their cognitive and physical needs. Such apps assist in day-to-day communication and foster learning and personal expression, providing a voice to those who might otherwise struggle to be heard.

Integrating these technologies into daily life can significantly enhance the user's ability to interact with the world around them. For example, incorporating an SGD into classroom settings can empower students to participate in discussions and express their understanding of the material, promoting a more inclusive learning environment. These devices can facilitate more straightforward communication with colleagues in the workplace, reducing misunderstandings and fostering a collaborative atmosphere. Socially, SGDs and mobile apps can help users engage more fully with friends and family, participate in conversations, and express their feelings more effectively, which enhances relationships and builds social confidence.

Practical tips for integrating these technologies include starting with familiar settings where the user feels comfortable and gradually introducing the devices in more public environments. Training sessions with caregivers, peers, and educators can also be invaluable. These sessions help the user become more proficient with the technology and educate others on interacting with the device, ensuring smoother and more meaningful communication. Additionally, many organizations and therapists offer workshops and training programs to help users and their support networks maximize the benefits of these technologies, making them powerful advocates for independence and inclusion.

Navigating the world of nonverbal communication technology opens possibilities for those who communicate differently. By leveraging these advanced tools, individuals can experience a greater sense of agency and connectivity, paving the way for more prosperous, more fulfilling interactions in every aspect of their lives. Whether at home, in educational settings, or within the community, these technologies provide a voice, offering a profound sense of empowerment that echoes across all areas of life.

EDUCATIONAL TOOLS FOR CONTINUOUS LEARNING

Education is not just about acquiring knowledge; it's about opening doors to new possibilities and understanding the world around us more clearly. For you, as an adult on the autism spectrum, the traditional educational models might not always align with your learning needs, which can make continuous learning seem daunting. Thankfully, technology has paved the way for learning environments that cater to diverse needs and preferences, making education more accessible and effective than ever before.

Online learning platforms have revolutionized how we learn, offering courses on virtually any topic, from computer programming to art history. These platforms, such as Coursera, Udemy, GameU, and Khan Academy, are particularly beneficial because they often allow you to learn at your own pace. This means you can take the time you need to fully understand the material without feeling rushed or pressured by the pace of others. Additionally, many of these courses offer visual teaching aids such as video lectures, interactive simulations, and infographics, which can be incredibly helpful if you find visual learning more engaging or easier to comprehend. For instance, if you're interested in learning about astronomy, watching a high-definition video that visually explains the concept of black holes might be more impactful than reading about them.

Furthermore, these platforms often feature community elements that enable you to connect with other learners who share your interests. This social learning aspect makes the learning process more enjoyable and allows you to exchange ideas and questions with peers worldwide, broadening your understanding and perspective on the subjects you are passionate about. This sense of community can help you feel more connected and less isolated, enhancing your learning experience.

Turning our focus to mobile apps, these tools have also made significant strides in catering to different learning styles, mainly through interactive and multimedia approaches. Apps like Quizlet allow you to create custom flashcards, a fantastic way to reinforce learning through repetition and active recall. For those who enjoy problem-solving, apps like Brilliant replace traditional learning methods with hands-on, interactive problem-solving scenarios in mathematics, science, and computer science, making learning more dynamic and engaging.

Technology can be crucial in adapting your learning environment to minimize distractions and maximize comfort. Noise-canceling headphones can be a game-changer if you find background noise distracting. Creating a quieter environment allows you to focus more intently on your studies without being continually pulled away by external sounds. Similarly, software solutions that adjust screen brightness and contrast can reduce visual strain, particularly during long study sessions. Tools like flux adjust your screen's display to the time of day, reducing blue light exposure in the evenings, which can help reduce eye strain and prevent sleep disruption.

Emphasizing the importance of lifelong learning and personal development, technology opens a world where education is not confined to classrooms or specific life stages. It offers a pathway to continuous growth and development, accessible from the comfort of your home or even on the go. Engaging with these tools keeps your mind sharp and empowers you to take charge of your personal and professional growth at any stage. The flexibility and variety provided by online platforms and apps ensure that learning can remain a lifelong adventure full of discovery and enrichment.

Integrating these technological tools into your educational pursuits sets you up for success in a world where knowledge and adaptability are key. Whether you're looking to advance in your career, start a new hobby, or learn something new, the resources are at your fingertips, ready to help you expand your horizons and embrace the joy of learning.

Sensory-Friendly Gadgets and How to Use Them

Finding solace in sensory-friendly gadgets can be a game-changer in a world that often feels overwhelmingly noisy and unbearably bright. These devices, designed with sensory needs, can significantly enhance your daily life, making environments more manageable and less anxiety-inducing. Let's explore some of the most valuable gadgets available and discuss how to customize and integrate them into your routines for a smoother, more comfortable day-to-day experience.

When managing sensory sensitivities, the right gadgets can make all the difference. White noise machines, for instance, are invaluable for those who need a consistent auditory backdrop to mask disruptive noises. Whether it's the unpredictable sounds of city traffic or the sudden clangs that might occur in a household, a white noise machine can provide a steady, soothing sound that helps maintain calm. Similarly, wearable sensory devices such as weighted vests or compression clothing can offer constant, gentle pressure that many find comforting, like a reassuring hug.

Lighting, too, plays a crucial role in sensory regulation. Lighting systems that adjust based on the time of day or your mood can help create an environment that supports your sensory preferences. For example, lights that dim gradually as the evening sets in can signal your body that it's time to wind down, reducing anxiety and aiding in the transition to bedtime. These systems can often be programmed to change colors; soft blues or greens might be soothing during a stressful workday, while warmer tones can make a living space feel cozy and inviting.

Customizing these devices to suit your specific needs can significantly enhance their effectiveness. Many sensory devices have settings that can be adjusted to suit individual preferences. For example, a white noise machine might have various sound options like ocean waves, rain, or static. Experimenting with different settings to find what best soothes you is key. For lighting systems, adjusting the intensity and color of the lights to match your activity level throughout the day can help regulate your mood and energy levels. Many modern systems are smartphone-compatible, allowing you to adjust right from your phone, crafting the perfect sensory environment with just a few taps.

Integrating these gadgets into your daily routine can help ensure your environment is always attuned to your sensory needs. Place a white noise machine in your workspace to help you focus during the day and in your bedroom to improve your sleep quality at night. Wear compression clothing under your regular clothes if you find daily commutes stressful, or use a weighted lap pad while sitting at your desk or dining table. Lighting systems can be programmed to change at various times of the day: softer, cooler lights to stimulate wakefulness in the morning and warmer, dimmer lights to signal that it's time to prepare for rest.

While the benefits of using these sensory-friendly gadgets are immense, including increased comfort and decreased anxiety, it's essential to consider factors such as cost and maintenance. Investing in durable and easy-to-maintain high-quality products can ensure they remain functional and beneficial in the long run. Also, finding the right balance of sensory input is crucial. Too much reliance on gadgets can be as overwhelming as the sensory input they're meant to mitigate. It's about finding what works best for you, which might mean using these devices during specific parts of your day or for activities that you find challenging.

Managing life with sensory sensitivities can often feel like trying to calm a sea of endless waves. But with the right tools—tools that you can adjust and control—you can create islands of calm in your daily ocean. These gadgets provide immediate relief from sensory overload and empower you to take charge of your environment, making the world less overwhelming and more navigable.

As we close this chapter on making the most of technology, it's clear that these tools offer more than convenience—they provide a pathway to enhanced self-awareness and autonomy. The ability to tailor technology to meet personal needs is empowering, giving you the confidence to engage with the world on your terms. Looking ahead, the next chapter of your life will build on this foundation, exploring strategies for maintaining mental and emotional well-being in a world that doesn't always align with your needs. By continuing to leverage technology and other resources, you can forge a path that not only navigates but also enriches the landscape of adult autism.

CONCLUSION

As we reach the final pages of our shared journey, I want to take a moment to reflect on the paths we've navigated together. From unraveling the complexities of autism in adulthood, enhancing communication skills, and forging meaningful relationships to mastering daily living skills, managing sensory challenges, and prioritizing your mental health, this book has been a guide through the terrain of life's challenges and triumphs. We've explored how to advocate for ourselves, connect with supportive communities, delve into our interests, and harness the power of technology to create a life that accommodates and celebrates your unique perspective.

At the heart of our discussions has been a central, empowering message: Neurodiversity is a profound strength. Your ability to see the world through an alternative lens isn't just a trait; it's a superpower that can bring creativity, insight, and sensitivity to your interactions and endeavors.

Embracing this perspective shifts the narrative from overcoming a deficit to leveraging distinct advantages.

Here are some key insights to carry with you:

- Understanding and advocating for your needs leads to more fulfilling interactions and experiences.
- Building and maintaining relationships are about communication, mutual understanding, and respect for each other's uniqueness.
- Daily living skills enhance independence and confidence, empowering you to take charge of your life.
- Recognizing and managing sensory inputs can profoundly affect your comfort and success in various environments.
- Continuously seeking knowledge and personal growth enriches your life and prepares you for new challenges.

I encourage you to take these strategies and insights and make them your own. Apply them in ways that feel right for you and take proactive steps toward crafting a life that understands and embraces your individuality. Remember, every small step is a leap toward a more confident and empowered you.

Thank you sincerely for walking this path with me. Knowing that you have chosen to engage with this book fills me with gratitude and deep connection. You are definitely not alone on this journey. There's a whole community out there that gets it, understands the challenges, and celebrates the victories alongside you.

Stay curious and open to learning. Life is an ever-evolving landscape, and maintaining a spirit of discovery will keep you adaptable and prepared to meet its changes. Your journey doesn't end here; it evolves daily as you grow and adapt.

I invite you to share your story with others. Whether through online platforms, in local support groups, or within your circle of friends and family, your experiences have power. They deepen communal bonds, foster understanding, and pave the way for others to navigate similar paths.

Looking forward, I'm optimistic about a future where neurodiversity is accepted and valued for the richness it brings to our collective human experience. Let's continue to advocate for a world that recognizes and celebrates the diverse ways our minds work. Together, we can contribute to a broader conversation about inclusion and the beauty of seeing the world from many different perspectives.

Here's to moving forward, to growing together, and to a world that appreciates every spectrum of the human mind. May this book serve as a stepping stone toward that vibrant, inclusive future.

Now, you have the tools to achieve your goals in life and the knowledge to show other readers where to get this information.

Simply by leaving your honest opinion of this book on Amazon, you'll show others seeking help in the autism spectrum area where they can find the information they are looking for and share your passion for improving their lives.

Thank you for being so helpful. Autism awareness is kept alive when we pass on our knowledge, and you're helping me to do just that.

Scan the QR code to leave your review:

REFERENCES

"Americans with Disabilities Act Fact Sheet." n.d. Autism Society. https://autismsociety.org/wp-content/uploads/2021/11/ADA-Fact-Sheet-1-1.pdf.

Arky, Beth. "Treating Sensory Processing Issues." Child Mind Institute, n.d. https://childmind.org/article/treating-sensory-processing-issues/.

Assistive Technology & Me. "Apps for Adults with Autism Spectrum Disorders," August 13, 2020. https://www.atandme.com/accessible-apps/apps-for-adults-with-autism-spectrum-disorders/.

Autism Alliance of Michigan. "A Guide on Self Advocacy," April 7, 2023. https://autismallianceofmichigan.org/a-guide-to-self-advocacy/.

Autism Society. "Autism Society Creating Connections for the Autism Community to Live Fully.," n.d. https://autismsociety.org/.

Autism Speaks. "Financial Planning Tool Kit," n.d. https://www.autismspeaks.org/tool-kit/financial-planning-tool-kit.

Benley, Ross. "Modifying Your Home for Sensory-Sensitive Individuals (2024)." Architectural Digest, March 9, 2023. https://www.architecturaldigest.com/reviews/home-improvement/sensory-processing-disorder.

Brewer, Rebecca, Murphy, Jennifer, and Spectrum. "People with Autism Can Read Emotions, Feel Empathy." Scientific American, n.d. https://www.scientificamerican.com/article/people-with-autism-can-read-emotions-feel-empathy1/.

CCC-A, Kristie Brown Lofland, M. S. "Evidence-Based Practices for Effective Communication and Social Intervention: Articles: Indiana Resource Center for Autism: Indiana University Bloomington." Indiana Resource Center for Autism, n.d. https://iidc.indiana.edu/irca/articles/evidence-based-practices-for-effective-communication-and-social-intervention.html.

Elwan, Yasmin. "Online Forums: Your Gateway to Knowledge and Community." *Internet Safety Statistics* (blog), March 27, 2024. https://www.internetsafetystatistics.com/navigating-world-online-forums/.

Everyday Speech. "Exploring the Role of Tone of Voice in Effective Communication," August 21, 2023. https://everydayspeech.com/sel-implementation/exploring-the-role-of-tone-of-voice-in-effective-communication/.

Family, Helping Hands. "Mealtime Tips and Recipes for Kids with Autism." Helping Hands Family, September 12, 2022. https://hhfamily.com/mealtime-tips-and-recipes-for-kids-with-autism/.

"FAQ SHEET STARTING AN AUTISM SUPPORT/ SELF-ADVOCACY GROUP." n.d. Autism Services, Education, Resources, and Training Collaborative (ASERT). https://paautism.org/wp-content/uploads/2021/02/StartingAnAutismSupportGroup.pdf.

Gallagher, Anne Marie. "What Are the Advantages of a Late Autism Spectrum Disorder (ASD) Diagnosis?" Connect To Autism, January 6, 2020. https://connecttoautism.org/what-are-the-advantages-of-a-late-autism-spectrum-disorder-asd-diagnosis/.

Ghanouni, Parisa, and Stephanie Quirke. "Resilience and Coping Strategies in Adults with Autism Spectrum Disorder." *Journal of Autism and Developmental Disorders* 53, no. 1 (2023): 456–67. https://doi.org/10.1007/s10803-022-05436-y.

Hill, Jessica. "The Ultimate Guide to Sensory Diets - Activities, Templates, and More." Harkla, July 8, 2022. https://harkla.co/blogs/special-needs/sensory-diet.

Jacobi, Collin. "Coping Skills for Adults with Sensory Processing Disorder." *Covey* (blog), December 6, 2023. https://covey.org/coping-skills-for-sensory-processing-disorder/.

Laushman, Patty. "How Autistic Individuals Can Improve Active Listening Skills." ThriveAutismCoaching, December 6, 2023. https://www.thriveautismcoaching.com/post/how-autistic-individuals-can-improve-active-listening-skills.

Lehman, Kathryn. "Autism and Time Management | Autism Speaks," n.d. https://www.autismspeaks.org/expert-opinion/autism-time-management.

Maddox, Brenna B., Kelsey S. Dickson, Nicole A. Stadnick, David S. Mandell, and Lauren Brookman-Frazee. "Mental Health Services for Autistic Individuals Across the Lifespan: Recent Advances and Current Gaps." *Current Psychiatry Reports* 23, no. 10 (August 17, 2021): 66. https://doi.org/10.1007/s11920-021-01278-0.

McEvoy, Kenna. "Top Strategies for Supporting Time Management for Those With Autism." Stages Learning, n.d. https://blog.stageslearning.com/blog/top-strategies-for-supporting-time-management-for-those-with-autism.

National Autistic Society. "Making Friends - a Guide for Autistic Adults," n.d. https://www.autism.org.uk/advice-and-guidance/topics/family-life-and-relationships/making-friends/autistic-adults.

Parkhurst, Emma. "How Hobbies Improve Mental Health." Utah State University, October 25, 2021. https://extension.usu.edu/mentalhealth/articles/how-hobbies-improve-mental-health.

Prakash, Rewant. "Use of Assistive Technology to Address the Overwhelming Sensory Stimuli in Individuals with Autism...." *Medium* (blog), September 6, 2018. https://medium.com/@rewantprakash/use-of-assistive-technology-to-address-the-overwhelming-sensory-stimuli-in-individuals-with-autism-67f13c7a6604.

Reid, Sheldon. "Adult Autism and Relationships." HelpGuide.org, April 9, 2022. https://www.helpguide.org/mental-health/autism/adult-autism-and-relationships.

Rex, Bright. "Breaking Down Barriers: Building Inclusive Online Communities." *Medium* (blog), March 1, 2024. https://medium.com/meeds-dao/breaking-down-barriers-building-inclusive-online-communities-78b4e10ae379.

Romualdez, Anna Melissa, Brett Heasman, Zachary Walker, Jade Davies, and Anna Remington. "'People Might Understand Me Better': Diagnostic Disclosure Experiences of Autistic Individuals in the Workplace." *Autism in Adulthood* 3, no. 2 (June 1, 2021): 157–67. https://doi.org/10.1089/aut.2020.0063.

Seeberger, Christel. "What Is a Sensory-Friendly Environment?" Sensory Friendly Solutions, August 15, 2021. https://www.sensoryfriendly.net/what-is-a-sensory-friendly-environment/.

Sharon Kaye-O'Connor. "How to Find a Neurodiversity-Affirming Therapist." Choosing Therapy, August 4, 2024. https://www.choosingtherapy.com/find-a-neurodiversity-affirming-therapist/#:

Synapse. "Autism, PDD-NOS & Asperger's Fact Sheets | Guide to Body Language for Adults on the Autism Spectrum," n.d. https://www.autism-help.org/adults-aspergers-body-language.htm#:

"Technology and Autism | Autism Speaks," n.d. https://www.autismspeaks.org/technology-and-autism.

The Carmen B. Pingree Autism Center of Learning. "10 Best Sensory Toys for Children with Autism," August 28, 2020. https://carmenbpingree.com/blog/best-sensory-toys-for-children-with-autism/.

UDS Foundation. "How to Volunteer with People with Disabilities," May 27, 2022. https://udservices.org/how-to-volunteer-with-people-with-disabilities/.

"Understanding Executive Function Difficulties." n.d. BASS Autism Service for Adults. https://autismwales.org/wp-content/uploads/2020/09/10-Skills-for-Life-Handout.pdf.

Worley, Rachel. "5 Autistic Professionals Share Their Networking Tips – Xceptional," November 17, 2020. https://xceptional.io/employees/5-autistic-professionals-share-networking-tips/.

Made in the USA
Middletown, DE
08 June 2025

76691445R00113